THE PROMISE
OF
DISCIPLESHIP

THE PROMISE

OF

DISCIPLESHIP

NEAL A. MAXWELL

DESERET
BOOK

SALT LAKE CITY, UTAH

Printed in the United States of America   72082-6833

10   9   8   7   6   5   4   3   2   1

CONTENTS

ACKNOWLEDGMENTS

Special appreciation is due to several. First, as always, I am grateful to my wife, Colleen, for providing not only the deference of time and schedule required for me to try to write, such as in the summer and Christmas holidays, but especially for her steady, exemplary ways of discipleship, so worthy of my contemplation. Then, to our only son, Cory, who encouraged this effort both personally and professionally, and his colleague Suzanne Brady, who did careful editing so deserving of thanks.

Susan Jackson speedily and accurately did the necessary things, including the finding of filed fragments and quotations. While the manuscript was in its rough-draft form, two friends, William O. Nelson and H. E. "Bud" Scruggs, gave helpful commentary from differing perspectives. Larry Skidmore was good to track down quotations from earlier Church leaders when their words were only partially remembered by me.

There is an entire group, however, not identifiable by name, who deserve appreciation, too. These members of the Church, whom I call high-yield and low-maintenance members, constantly provide the rest of us with their own quiet and steady examples of discipleship.

I alone am responsible for what appears in this book. It is *not* an official Church publication. Even so, I hope it will assist members and others who take any of their time to peruse it.

PREAMBLE

So often my writings have turned in one way or another to the continuing challenge and adventure of discipleship. To ask why is a fair question.

First of all, discipleship is the fundamental process in which we are to be "anxiously engaged" (D&C 58:27). Furthermore, only discipleship—"follow me"—connects beliefs and behavior, focusing on what we are becoming as well as what we are thinking and doing. Thus, discipleship cannot be merely intellectual. Did not Jesus prescribe and describe this convergence by saying, "Take my yoke upon you, and learn of me?" (Matthew 11:29). Moreover, the deepest development of discipleship occurs only in this particular manner, small though our yokes may be compared to His.

True, so very many in the world don't even know about Jesus, let alone know enough to respond to the question, "What think ye of Christ?" (Matthew 22:42). Additionally, of those who are aware of Him, many are desensitized and diverted, because He is "far from the thoughts and intents of [their] hearts" (Mosiah 5:13). But genuine Latter-day Saints clearly know who He is and, further, that building up His kingdom is what we are to do "first" (JST Matthew 6:38). No true disciple can be distant from his Master anyway: Christ alone marks the way perfectly. Amid life's uncertainties, His summoning trumpet always gives a certain sound.

Meanwhile, the distracting and intruding things of the world press upon us. In their times and moments, these things are often powerful, even prevailing, in the lives of many. These cares can preoccupy us, if we let them. Whatever these external tugs and pulls are, however, and whatever their lures and perks, the things of the world do not compare to the adventure of discipleship, the trek of treks. Furthermore, serious discipleship is ripe with joyful promise.

But this trek is a difficult, even rugged, journey at times. A great abundance of available spiritual direction and nutrition is needed for this trek. The harvest of the Restoration is truly "enough and to spare," just as the Lord said of the earth's resources (D&C 104:17).

A virtual lifetime of study has long since fully persuaded me that Jesus' gospel is, indeed, an inexhaustible gospel. It has proved to be even more exciting in my sunset years, when age itself might have dulled my interests. The gospel invites scrutiny by study, and it induces the on-going introspection necessary for genuine discipleship. Whenever we can help each other along the path of discipleship by words, deeds, and examples, we truly bless each other.

The chapters to follow, therefore, concern the relevancy of the Restoration for our time, its abundance, and the attributes of God on which we constantly depend and which we are to emulate. There are also some samplings of "all these things" which constitute the stiff, tutorial challenges but bring much joy. Because the gifts of the Holy Ghost are so significant, these are given more attention than I have ever given them before, though still not enough.

The book likewise invites us to cast our minds forward to the adventure awaiting us all in the spirit world, where the Lord's work continues with even greater scope and intensity. Finally, a different salute is made to the Prophet Joseph Smith out of deep appreciation for what he accomplished while serving as the Prophet of the Restoration. Try as they have—and will—Joseph's detractors will never dissolve the loyalty of the vast majority of members, for the promise is that "thy people shall never be turned against thee by the testimony of traitors" (D&C 122:3).

As is my custom, extensive use is made of the scriptures throughout this book. In the abundance of Restoration scriptures are some which produce a sense of wonder. These scriptures are not drenched in detail; they give, instead, bare-bones but vital information, such as about the demographics of dissent expressed in the premortal world: "And also a third part of the hosts of heaven turned he [the devil] away from me because of their agency" (D&C 29:36).

Likewise, a declaratory revelation about the nature of the Holy Ghost comes in a terse verse: "The Father has a body of flesh and bones as tangible as man's; the Son also; but the Holy Ghost has not a body of flesh and bones, but is a personage of Spirit" (D&C 130:22). Very essential information is thus often given but without elaboration!

Other gospel gems, however, give us important salvational data, while simultaneously disclosing tender and insightful things about prophetic personalities. Such was surely the case with eloquent Jacob, as he taught regarding the chastity and fidelity required by the seventh commandment:

"Wherefore, it burdeneth my soul that I should be constrained, because of the strict commandment which I have received from God, to admonish you according to your crimes, to enlarge the wounds of those who are already wounded, instead of consoling and healing their wounds; and those who have not been wounded, instead of feasting upon the pleasing word of God have daggers placed to pierce their souls and wound their delicate minds" (Jacob 2:9).

Equally eloquent is Enoch's splendid, self-revelatory, and extensive conversation with the Lord, descriptive not only of His doctrine, character, and emotion, but of the Lord as well:

"And it came to pass that the God of heaven looked upon the residue of the people, and he wept; and Enoch bore record of it, saying: How is it that the heavens weep, and shed forth their tears as the rain upon the mountains?" (Moses 7:28).

There is no parallel to that disclosure of divine emotion known to me, and what follows it is drenched in doctrine as well.

There are verses of scripture which teach while reflecting linguistic loveliness but without major doctrinal elaboration, such as this lamentation over human disregard for spiritual wisdom:

"Yea, they are as a wild flock which fleeth from the shepherd, and scattereth, and are driven, and are devoured by the beasts of the forest" (Mosiah 8:21).

Important insights about discipleship are embodied and conveyed in beautiful but succinct ways as in this inspired but haunting interrogatory which deals with the essence of failed discipleship:

"For how knoweth a man the master whom he has not served, and who is a stranger unto him, and is far from the thoughts and intents of his heart?" (Mosiah 5:13).

Alas, many stay at arm's length from Him whose arm is outstretched.

Furthermore, one notices in searching the feast-filled array of scriptures a side-by-sideness, such as when a fleeting geographical fact is juxtaposed with a verse of keen, spiritual importance concerning discipleship:

"And it came to pass that they did multiply and prosper

exceedingly in the land of Helam; and they built a city, which they called the city of Helam" (Mosiah 23:20).

A geographical place is noted for reasons known to the Lord but is clearly not salvationally significant to us. Verse 21, however, is obviously vital for us as disciples to know, because it frames the realistic expectations we should have about discipleship:

"Nevertheless the Lord seeth fit to chasten his people; yea, he trieth their patience and their faith."

Thus, while many Restoration verses have doctrinal richness as well as richness of expression, some constitute revelations without elaboration. In developmental discipleship, the scriptures are, therefore, of inestimable worth.

By having and applying "the key of knowledge"—"the fulness of the scriptures"—we accelerate our journey of discipleship (JST Luke 11:53). Less appreciated is the fact that good behavior brings more knowledge (2 Peter 1:8). Again, happy convergence is found in discipleship.

As to the entirety of the Restoration, an introductory caveat is given about the provincialness displayed by most of us in the midst of the enriching expansiveness of all that is now had again.

Given its intellectual range of components, no wonder we believers are still inventorying the harvest basket of the Restoration! Having dashed about the wonder-filled landscape of the Restoration, exclaiming and observing, we should not be surprised if some of our first impressions prove to be more childish than definitive. Brushing against such tall timber inevitably leaves the scent of pine upon us. Our pockets are filled with souvenir cones and colorful rocks, and we are filled with almost childish glee.

There is no way to grasp it all. Little wonder some of us regard a particular tree as if it were the whole of the forest.

Or, that in our exclamations, there are some unintended exaggerations. We have seen far too much to describe fully. Indeed, we "cannot say the smallest part which [we] feel" (Alma 26:16).

Yet by seeing things with "an eye of faith" and with the help of the Spirit, we really can better see "things as they really are" and better make our way along the path of discipleship (Ether 12:19; Jacob 4:13).

The times in which we live, however, are and will be such that "all things shall be in commotion" (D&C 88:91). Hope is so much needed in such times, acknowledging thereby the "divine determination" by means of which God brings His purposes fully to pass. To ensure this outcome, our Loving Father has certainly made "ample provision."[1]

No wonder the greatness of our message should be matched by the meekness of its bearers. We cannot be mute about the message, but we must be truly humble. In our individual discipleship, we need to be capable of spiritual enlargement without swollen hypocrisy (D&C 121:42).

The gospel's strong and stretching framework is matched by its interior consistency: it is striking in its richness and relevance. The gospel of Jesus Christ is not a collection of random aphorisms or of unconnected epigrams. It is a combination of truth, power, and beauty with some truths as stark as they are reassuring.

The requirements of the gospel of Jesus Christ are not simply an arbitrary set of duties designed to make us jump through certain hoops in order to please God. In fact, Christ's teachings and covenants mark the only true way Home. The commandments help us to live "after the manner of happiness" (2 Nephi 5:24). God, Who knows all things, knows the nature of true happiness. Moreover, He wants His children to have all the happiness we truly desire and choose—here and now as well as in the there and then.

The prophetic exclamation "O how great the plan of our God!" is as summational as it is exclamational (2 Nephi 9:13). The very existence of such a "great" plan of happiness should strike us more forcibly and indelibly than it often does. Yet we mortals sometimes strangely resent the means provided to reach that glorious end.

Some may say of the doctrines of the kingdom that they too are daunting and demanding. They do require real faith.

Have not most parents stood in a swimming pool urging their frightened child to trust them, as that child waits anxiously on an edge? Parents earnestly seek to reassure, saying, "Don't worry! I'll catch you!" The child's understandable anxiety is fully answered in Enoch's reassuring words about a loving and rescuing Father God: "Yet thou art there" (Moses 7:30).

He is!

CHAPTER

1

"ALL THINGS SHALL BE IN COMMOTION"

A striking and repeated prophecy declares that in the last days "the whole earth shall be in commotion"; indeed, "all things shall be in commotion" (D&C 45:26; 88:91; see also Luke 21:9). Clearly this will include seismic and physical shakings, as Elder Bruce R. McConkie observed:

"One of the signs of the times is that the elements (meaning weather conditions and such things as bring about earthquakes and the like) shall be in commotion in the last days. (D&C 88:87–92.)."[1]

Yet while including such physical disruptiveness, the commotion and unsettlement will go beyond Richter readings. Elder James E. Talmage so observed in general conference in 1918:

"Have you never read that all things should be in commotion in these the last days? This is the day of shaking, when everything that can be shaken shall be shaken, and only those things which are established upon an eternal foundation shall endure."[2]

It will take the rivets of the Restoration to keep things from sliding, because the commotion includes not only the geophysical but also the geometric swings away from traditional moral values. Vertigo as to values brings a special dizziness.

In today's relativistic society, we see indulgence masquerading as tolerance. We see the primacy of the "politically correct" substituting for righteous indignation and for moral outrage. Instead of genuine and pervasive concern for the public good, we see intense devotion paid to niche causes. People are often viewed as advocates of causes rather than as neighbors, being stereotyped because of their interest groups. It is anemic enough to know neighbors and others only as functions but worse still to regard them so much more narrowly. Because all others are actually the spirit sons and daughters of God, the new math of the new morality is even more disturbing than it is fuzzy.

It is sometimes said, in spite of media and market hype, that most people quietly go on living decent lives, unaffected by the wave of enticements and inducements flowing from a carnal world. Furthermore, there is a reassuring scripture:

"Now it is not common that the voice of the people desireth anything contrary to that which is right; but it is common for the lesser part of the people to desire that which is not right; therefore this shall ye observe and make it your law—to do your business by the voice of the people" (Mosiah 29:26).

Significantly and subsequently, however, the voice of the people can be eroded and corrupted:

"For as their laws and their governments were established by the voice of the people, and they who chose evil were more numerous than they who chose good, therefore they were ripening for destruction, for the laws had become corrupted" (Helaman 5:2; see also Alma 10:19–20).

Thus, wrongheaded ways can affect more than just those in spiritual swing districts. Any separating membranes are not impermeable, and families are especially at risk from commotion as to values.

If from birth, as in Sodom and Gomorrah, the rising generation is so inundated by the worst of worldliness, what chance do they have, given such conditioning? (Genesis 18:22–23). No wonder, therefore, that through the ages prophets have raised warning voices. It isn't just those at the margins who are at risk—it is society itself!

Whatever the nature of the surrounding commotion, however, Jesus' calming counsel to his followers remains "be not terrified" (Luke 21:9). General anxiety will still be high, and "men's hearts shall fail them" (D&C 45:26). Additionally, there will be "distress of nations, with perplexity" (Luke 21:25). Old-fashioned fear will be pervasive, amid which confusion discipleship will be increasingly demanding (D&C 88:91).

In any case, we have been soberingly advised of our latter-day time: "Behold, the enemy is combined" (D&C 38:12). Encompassing, not random and occasional evil, will finally be the challenge. Yet true disciples can "be of good cheer" (D&C 61:36). Furthermore, some of the turbulence will be redemptive: "For the kingdom of the devil must shake, and they which belong to it must needs be stirred up unto repentance, or the devil will grasp them with his everlasting chains, and they be stirred up to anger, and perish" (2 Nephi 28:19).

Whatever the conglomerate nature of the challenge, it will be of sufficient length and intensity to create some disgorging dissonance, disturbing some especially:

"But it is they who do not fear me, neither keep my commandments . . . and all those that do wickedly and build up the kingdom of the devil—yea, verily, verily, I say unto you, that it is they that I will disturb, and cause to tremble and shake to the center" (D&C 10:56).

At the same time, however, others will be contrastingly "stirred up to anger," for "at that day shall [Satan] rage in the hearts of the children of men, and stir them up to anger against that which is good" (2 Nephi 28:19–20). Isaiah foresaw the time when evil would be called good and good evil (Isaiah 5:20; 2 Nephi 15:20).

The word *rage* will not prove to be an understatement. An accompanying tactic will be to cause those of little faith to "fear . . . persecution" (D&C 40:2). A contrasting tactic will be to "pacify" and "lull" vulnerable members of the Church (2 Nephi 28:21). Hence, the stirrings will swirl diversely.

There is still much good wheat growing among the seeming tares, however; hence, stereotyping others serves us poorly. Hence, too, the Lord's restraint in coming down in final judgment (D&C 38:12; 86:5). Therefore, we should act wisely lest we judge prematurely or act amiss. Besides, the difficult last days will be shortened for the "elect's sake" (Matthew 24:22; Mark 13:20; Joseph Smith–Matthew 1:20; JST Matthew 24:20).

From such churnings and tumblings, some souls will come into the kingdom bruised but believing. Having made their way courageously through guerilla territory, they will be searching heroically for spiritual liberty—even as forces in the world are relentlessly seeking "to overthrow the freedom of all lands, nations, and countries" (Ether 8:25). More commotion!

At some point, "the world and the wisdom thereof," the

pride of the world represented by the metaphoric "great and spacious building," will fall (1 Nephi 11:35–36). Whether in a sudden swoop or incrementally, the collapse will occur—resoundingly and visibly. More commotion!

Yet, as already noted, the roiling will create at least some redemptiveness in certain individuals presently insensitive to spiritual things, nagging doubts of their previous doubts, stirring them to consider gospel truths previously neglected or rejected by responding to that which they have "never considered" before, surely including the divinity of atoning Jesus and the reality of the Restoration. The latter constitutes what, beginning with Isaiah, scriptures call the Lord's "strange act" and "strange work" (D&C 101:94–95; Isaiah 28:21; 3 Nephi 20:45; 21:8).

Having been so described, the Lord's work will go against the conceptual and behavioral grain of much of society. The "restitution" of what is unfamiliar, uncommon, unusual, and unique will test perceptivity but will also be refreshing for those who receive it (Acts 3:19).

Without such refreshing vision, people do perish spiritually (Proverbs 29:18). To help individuals—including by helping them discern between righteousness and wickedness—God will pour "out [His] Spirit upon all flesh" (D&C 95:4; 101:95).

A fresh view is not always welcomed, being jarring to those who are intensely set in their ways. Sin enjoys its own status quo, too. Even the remarkable Enoch was not welcomed by many of his contemporaries. Of him and his labors, it was said anciently, "There is a strange thing in the land" (Moses 6:38).

The Lord speaks of our responsibility to "wise men and rulers" who need to "hear and know that which they have never considered" (D&C 101:94). With the added light brought to people, there is added hope for some emancipating realism.

Sincere, secular solutions to some human problems will nevertheless prove demonstrably ineffective, resulting in further "distress . . . , with perplexity" (Luke 21:25). Besides, the basic cause of much despair has been clearly identified for us: "Despair cometh because of iniquity" (Moroni 10:22). The obvious and cumulative failures of the best laid plans of men—"the world and the wisdom thereof" (1 Nephi 11:35)—may jar some sufficiently to consider the Restoration's remedies never considered before (D&C 101:94).

Thus it is when things in our personal sector on this planet look grim, we especially need to have faith in a God who can successfully do His work and whose motives are those of a loving Father who desires to redeem His children.

Of course, there are moments when it is difficult for us to see how certain things can ever come to pass. Often our puzzlements are related to questions over God's timing, for He tells us repeatedly that He will do things "in mine own due time" (3 Nephi 20:29; 1 Nephi 10:3; Ether 3:25). Even so, our human tendency is to impose our calendars and clocks as if these were to be a fixed overlay on God's divine plans when, in fact, a specific part of His divine determination is to do things in His own due time as well as in His own way.

Meanwhile, the worldly gravitate toward those things which involve power, authority, ease, and riches—"the vain things of the world" (3 Nephi 6:15). God's word is of little interest to them; hence, most of them find it difficult to be "humble . . . because of the word" (Alma 32:14). Yet some may be sufficiently humbled because of compelling events.

Along with the general commotion, a few defectors and

dissidents occasionally vex us as they hyperventilate over their particular concerns; however, it is primarily the engulfing effects of a deteriorating world pressing on Church members which constitutes the most clear and present danger. "Evils and designs" really do operate through "conspiring [individuals] in the last days," and the clever "enemy is combined" (D&C 89:4; 38:12). By ourselves, we are no match. Furthermore, we can sometimes be victimized by different mobs.

There is such a thing as a subtle mob of bystanders—not a mob that cries aloud, "Barrabas," nor a mob that obviously holds the cloak of those who are throwing stones (Matthew 27:21; Acts 7:58). Rather, it is a different kind of mob, one which cleverly goes along with a bad trend and even goads on the activists and egoists, seeming not to care what the wrongdoer does as long as he is smooth and cool. Worse still, such subtle mobs are a collection of silent proxy givers. The onlookers might not actually do themselves what the offender does, but they enjoy the vicarious emotions without sensing any seeming accountability. Moreover, such enablers can then quickly slink away when the apogee of acting out is over.

Yet Church members must not be intimidated or lose composure amid the commotion, including seeing once morally unacceptable behavior become acceptable; nevertheless, "be not terrified" (Luke 21:9). One of the most subtle forms of intimidation is the gradual normalization of sinful aberration. Alexander Pope so cautioned:

> Vice is a monster of so frightful mien,
> As to be hated needs but to be seen;
> Yet seen too oft, familiar with her face,
> We first endure, then pity, then embrace.[3]

14

When something is wrong, increasing its commonality cannot really confer respectability.

Aleksandr Solzhenitsyn lamented recently, "If state, party and social policy will not be based on morality, then mankind has no future to speak of."[4]

With the enemy "combined" (D&C 38:12), it is vital to do all we can to keep ourselves and other members "in the right way" (Moroni 6:4). When the storms come, including "every wind of doctrine" (Ephesians 4:14), orthodoxy in both thought and behavior brings safety as well as felicity. Happily, amid such winds, the Holy Ghost not only helps us to recognize plain truth but also plain nonsense.

Patience and faith will keep us on the path of duty, even though "all things shall be in commotion" (D&C 88:91). Yes, turbulence will still take its toll on the faith and patience of some. Yes, commotion may erode and reduce the gospel commitments of some. But this kingdom, "a marvelous work and a wonder," will roll on, gathering a marvelous momentum (2 Nephi 27:26; 1 Nephi 22:8; D&C 4:1).

Parents should be especially cautious, however, about adding unintentionally to the daily commotion which swirls about them and their children. Our homes should be sanctuaries of peace and love. If we add to daily hecticness unnecessarily by overmuch involvement in outside activities, we can lose the special benefits of home. Parents are much more apt to be appreciated by their children as parents than as taxi drivers.

Once when Nephite members were understandably afraid, the prophet spoke to them and "hushed their fears" (Mosiah 23:28). King Hezekiah played a similar role for ancient Israel (2 Kings 18). Perhaps such may be necessary again in our time!

The last days of commotion will parallel some things as

"in the days of Noah" (Joseph Smith–Matthew 24:37). Because of the Restoration, we know more about the dark days in Noah's time. Biblically, we know the earth was "corrupt before God" and "filled with violence" and that "as the days of Noe were, so shall also the coming of the Son of man be" (Genesis 6:11; Matthew 24:37). Such indicators are important. While, back then, wickedness accumulated "in process of time" (Genesis 4:3), the destroying flood came with some suddenness. In the destruction of Sodom and Gomorrah, cumulative and gathering wickedness was likewise followed by suddenness. It will be so at the Lord's second coming, arriving, thief-like, "upon you unawares" (Luke 21:34; Matthew 24:37–38; Revelation 3:3). "For as a snare shall it come on all them that dwell on the face of the whole earth" (Luke 21:34–35; see also D&C 45:26).

In Noah's time, people were preoccupied with everyday living, such as eating and drinking, giving and receiving in marriage, suggesting the sometimes sedating role of routineness (Matthew 24:37–39).

Peter speaks of how the "longsuffering of God waited in the days of Noah" (1 Peter 3:20). Finally, the wickedness then exceeded that among all God's creations (Moses 7:36). A very cruel society existed, one "without affection" and "hat[ing] their own blood," not unlike the gross decadence in the post-Christ Nephite society (Moses 7:33; Moroni 9). In fact, when Enoch foresaw the sobering and overwhelming wickedness in the days of Noah, Enoch's distress was at first so great he "refused to be comforted" (Moses 7:44).

From certain apocryphal writings,[5] we receive interesting commentary about later and emerging conditions:

"In those days, the nations shall be confounded. . . . In those days, they (the women) shall become pregnant, but

16

they (the sinners) shall come out and abort their infants and cast them out from their midst" (1 Enoch 99:4–5).

"For in his days there will be a great confusion on the earth. . . . And nation will wage war against nation. And all the earth will be filled with blood and with very evil confusion. Even more than that, they will abandon their Creator. . . . And the adversary will make himself great and will be delighted with their deeds" (2 Enoch 70:5–6).

"Those . . . who do not glorify God, who practice on the earth the sin which is against nature, which is child corruption . . . in the manner of Sodom" (2 Enoch 10:4).

We know from Jesus' prophecies and others' which are scriptural that coarseness and cruelty will be present again as "the love of many will wax cold" and "peace [will have been] taken from the earth" (Matthew 24:12; D&C 1:35).

President Brigham Young described the side-by-sideness of the wheat and tares:

"It was revealed to me in the commencement of this Church, that the Church would spread, prosper, grow and extend, and that in proportion to the spread of the Gospel among the nations of the earth, so would the power of Satan rise."[6]

With such general decay, society's institutions, which previously may have served reasonably well, will reflect the decay and the inversion of some values. There will likewise be an as yet undefined "great division" among the people (2 Nephi 30:10).

Faithful members of the Church can and will survive spiritually, if we honor and keep our covenants made at the time of baptism and in the holy temples. We can be on the right side during the "great division," if we do not mirror the world. We can make an affirmative difference in the world for the better, if we are righteously different from the world. Happily, there are so very many decent and wonderful people of all creeds and cultures who likewise strive to do so!

Anciently, a small band of Greeks bravely held a mountain pass at Thermopylae against overwhelming numbers of Persians. The Persians demanded surrender, threatening to darken the skies with their arrows. The gallant Spartans said, "So much the better, we shall fight in the shade."[7] Outnumbered disciples "armed with righteousness" (1 Nephi 14:14) may know equivalent circumstances, as the children of light move forward, even in darkening conditions.

Jesus provided helpful counsel through the Restoration scriptures. For example—

> When you hear of wars and commotion, "see that ye be not troubled" (Joseph Smith–Matthew 1:23).

> "Whoso treasureth up my word, shall not be deceived" (Joseph Smith–Matthew 1:37).

> Take the Holy Spirit as your guide (D&C 45:57).

> "Watch, therefore . . . be ye also ready" (Joseph Smith–Matthew 1:46, 48).

It must be so with us in the commotion-filled days preceding the coming of the Son of Man—as individuals and as a Church. There is surely more than adequate spiritual nourishment available to strengthen us through the bounteous Restoration.

CHAPTER

2

"ENOUGH AND TO SPARE"

In the topsy-turvy, commotion-filled last days, one of the great blessings of the restored gospel of Jesus Christ is its timeliness and also its directing and nurturing abundance. Like the earth's natural resources, which are "enough and to spare," the truths and doctrines of the gospel give us precious perspective (D&C 104:17). Thus, we know not only the essential truths but also the interconnections between the "weightier" and other things (Matthew 23:23).

The eminent historian Will Durant, who sorted out and described many facts and their comparative significance, noted the human need wherein "we want to seize the value and perspective of passing things, and so to pull ourselves up out of the maelstrom of daily circumstance. We want to know that the little things are little, and the big things are big, before it is too late; we want to see things now as they will seem forever—'in the light of eternity.'"[1]

In a time when there are "so many kinds of voices in the world," His sheep know Whose voice to heed (1 Corinthians 14:10; Alma 5:60). The few examples which follow underscore the Restoration's timeliness, abundance, and significance and are intended to reconnoiter and to highlight, not to pause and particularize. Yet, how can one forgo some exclamations, at least in headline form, such as over the expansiveness of the universe?

Before such spiritual realizations can be hastened, however, the Lord had to remove certain "stumbling blocks," including the pinched perspectives within which some view Christ (1 Nephi 14:1).

The central doctrine that Jesus is the Christ, the Atoning and Risen Redeemer, removes those stumbling blocks and restores the true perspective of eternity. Compared to Jesus and the Atonement, all else is subordinate, as the Prophet Joseph Smith taught:

"The fundamental principles of our religion are the testimony of the Apostles and Prophets, concerning Jesus Christ, that He died, was buried, and rose again the third day, and ascended into heaven; and all other things which pertain to our religion are only appendages to it."[2]

To know Jesus more and more is to experience His attributes. We thus draw closer by way of appreciation, admiration, and even adoration of Him. We truly accelerate knowing Him, as we become more like Him by means of our imperfect adulation.

His appearances, as in the First Vision and in 3 Nephi, are incredibly important in removing the stumbling block of uncertainty concerning His divinity, His resurrection, and His relationship to the Father. For instance, Jesus is actually the Lord of the universe; long before He was Jesus of Nazareth, He created "worlds without number" under the Father's direction (Moses 1:33; D&C 76:24).

One ancient stumbling block regarding Jesus was the expectation about how the rescuing Messiah would emancipate the people militarily and politically. Jesus was not that

kind of an emancipator. Therefore, His violation of expectations and His death were, for some, an unfulfilling stumbling
block. The Greeks, on the other hand, regarded the whole
idea of a resurrecting Messiah as foolishness. This very irony
had been prophesied (Isaiah 8:14; 1 Corinthians 1:23; 1
Peter 2:8; 2 Nephi 18:14). The Jews wanted a sign, and the
Greeks wanted wisdom (1 Corinthians 1:22–23). Among
other blessings, the Restoration answers key questions that
have preoccupied and tormented ecclesiastical councils in
centuries past.

For those sufficiently meek, the Restoration provides the
resolving remedy with its fulness and its greater and clearer
"views of Christ and the resurrection" (Alma 27:28). Thus,
the bright sun of the Restoration melts away the icy stumbling blocks of false doctrines, some frozen in place over long
centuries (1 Nephi 14:1; D&C 123:7–8).

Just as was foreseen, the scriptures of the Restoration,
fusing and growing together with the Bible, have resulted in
a "confounding of false doctrines" (2 Nephi 3:12) and "the
taking away of . . . stumbling blocks" (1 Nephi 14:1).
Because certain prejudices have encrusted mortal lives, men
need, as King Benjamin taught, to believe and trust in God,
who comprehends all things, while men do not (Mosiah
4:9). Some mortals, strangely, are reluctant to let God be
God! (Mosiah 27:31).

Even with the gospel's precious perspective and its provision of much-needed remedies, because of long-standing
stumbling blocks and because of the cares and anxieties of
the world, comparatively few individuals will finally hear.
This is not unlike the situation in which some of Galileo's
friends reportedly refused to look through his telescope; they
did not really want a larger and more accurate view of things.
Some do want the truth but only "in part" (D&C 49:2),

amid the boring hedonism or the "humdrum nihilism of everyday life."[3] Most of all, however, the Restoration provides us with the vital doctrines, ordinances, authority, and organization essential to salvation and exaltation. No wonder the Lord desires "that all that will hear may hear" and that "faith might increase in the earth" (D&C 1:11, 21).

We should keep in mind, however, the metaphor Jesus used about the harvest basket that was "pressed down, and shaken together, and running over" (Luke 6:38). Surely that metaphor describes the harvest of truths, including truths about God's capacity and determination to bring His purposes to pass. Does He not say to us so reassuringly, "I am able to do mine own work"—two times in two verses? (2 Nephi 27:20–21). Likewise, does He not call us to help with His work? Yet how can we help much except we are serious disciples?

The very idea of revelations and prophets continues to be a major stumbling block for many. The "restitution of all things" (Acts 3:21) includes the role of Joseph Smith as the Prophet of the Restoration. For some, alas, he remains a stumbling block.

Hear President Brigham Young: "The first Elders can recollect, when we commenced preaching 'Mormonism,' that present revelation and a Prophet of God on the earth were the great stumbling blocks to the people, were what we had to contend against, and were, seemingly, the most potent obstacles in our way to the introduction of the Gospel."[4]

President George Q. Cannon agreed: "There was a day in our history when it was considered a crime for us to believe in revelation from God. I do not know that that day is entirely past. There was a day in our history when it was considered very improper for us to believe in Prophets or Apostles—that is, to believe that they ought to be in the

Church. There was a time when we were indicted by a mob in its written proclamation for believing in miracles. . . . You have doubtless thought, all of you, about the character of the men whom Jesus chose to be His Apostles. They were men who were stumbling-blocks to their generation, for they did not belong to the popular classes. They were not learned men, they were not rich men—that is in the worldly sense of the word—they were not dignified men; and Jesus Himself, the Lord of life and of glory, was a constant stumbling-block to His generation."[5]

While in the midst of the stirring and shaking and the removing of stumbling blocks, the numerical harvest for the Church will increase more than most of us realize, yet, it will not be massive—at least as the world measures such things. Still, numerical growth will surely stretch us as a people in terms of what we are now used to. Nephi provided some demographic contours:

"I beheld the church of the Lamb of God, and its numbers were few, because of the wickedness and abominations; . . . nevertheless, I beheld that the church of the Lamb, who were the saints of God, were also upon all the face of the earth; and their dominions upon the face of the earth were small, because of the wickedness" (1 Nephi 14:12).

Even so, great things await, for "Nephi, beheld the power of the Lamb of God, that it descended upon the saints of the church of the Lamb, and upon the covenant people of the Lord, who were scattered upon all the face of the earth; and they were armed with righteousness and with the power of God in great glory" (1 Nephi 14:12, 14).

Serious disciples will be "scattered upon all the face of the earth," constituting all the leaven they can. The spiritual growth of the Church, therefore, will be even more significant than its numerical growth (D&C 105:31). Why?

Because the spiritual sanctification of Church members is more vital than their numerical multiplication.

The Restoration also reestablished the Lord's process of revelation with God and angels conversing with men, especially regarding the plan of salvation (Alma 12:28–30). This doctrinal diamond, bright with many facets, is rich with implications for daily life as well as for eternity. Accepting the truths about the plan of happiness provides the needed focus for those who have eyes but yet do not see. In the physical eye, an astigmatism occurs when light fails to converge or focus on the single point. No wonder some, unfocused, are forever "looking beyond the mark" (Jacob 4:14).

Our only chance is the help of the Holy Ghost, seeing things with the "eye of faith," and then evaluating things as if with "the mind of Christ" (1 Corinthians 2:16). Such spiritual symmetry is a great protection for us in a contextual situation in which "an exceedingly great many do stumble" (1 Nephi 13:29). Without simple faith and the necessary revelations, people do tend to put down the power and the miracles of God. No wonder the Restoration was needed and was to occur "in mine own power," bringing back "much of my gospel" (1 Nephi 13:34).

Amid doubt and confusion we are reassured that in the presence of God, "all things . . . past, present, and future, . . . are continually before [Him]" (D&C 130:7). This special circumstance forms what the Prophet Joseph Smith described as God's living in "one eternal 'now.'"[6] The gospel's deep doctrines really are time-spanning, just as we sing about how truth "steps o'er" the "limits of time."[7]

What a needed reassurance this is about God's capacity, especially since our mortal "now" is so very different from God's eternal "now." In fact, the mortal present can be genuinely puzzling and even painful—unless illuminated by restored and reassuring perspectives bestowed from the eternal now.

Since we are eternal beings presently living in time, it is sometimes much more than a whisper which tells us "you're a stranger here."[8] Embarked on a Homeward journey, we find the skies are often overcast with dark cloud cover, yet disciples will never mistake passing, local cloud cover for general darkness.

Given all we yet lack in our spiritual symmetry, no wonder God uses the little mortal time available, sometimes in compressed ways, to develop us during this brief, second estate (Abraham 3:26). This urgency means that there can be few recesses and certainly no lengthy sabbaticals. Even our deserved reveries must be interruptible in order to hasten God's relentless remodeling of souls.

Amid the vastness of God's creations, if we are meek, God's shaping personalness helps us to develop. He is in the details—not only of galaxies, DNA, and molecules—but, so importantly, in our own lives. He is overseeing individual births and deaths while somehow overseeing cosmic births and funerals, such as when one earth passes away and another is born (Moses 1:38).

Not only does the Book of Mormon constitute "Another Testament of Jesus Christ" but it also brings back many of the "plain and precious things" so sorely needed since the Restoration came to help faith "increase in the earth" (1 Nephi 13:29; D&C 1:21). This latter-day fulness necessarily includes much greater knowledge concerning God's plan of salvation, thus providing a framework for faith, so that life, vexing and puzzling at times, makes sufficient sense for us to strive.

We are helped, for example, to understand considerably better why God, who is perfect in His goodness and power, nevertheless allows evil and suffering in the world. This latter concern is no small cause of sincere puzzlement for many and even resentment for some. We in the Church have yet to digest the relevant doctrines fully, let alone appreciate all the harvest of restored doctrines along with their spiritual food value and implications for our spiritual nurturance.

For example, how long have Christian doctrines actually been taught and ordinances administered? Ever since Adam! In that sense, not only was he the "first man" (1 Corinthians 15:45) but also the first Christian:

"And thus the Gospel began to be preached, from the beginning, being declared by holy angels sent forth from the presence of God, and by his own voice, and by the gift of the Holy Ghost.

"And thus all things were confirmed unto Adam, by an holy ordinance, and the Gospel preached, and a decree sent forth, that it should be in the world, until the end thereof; and thus it was. Amen" (Moses 5:58–59).

Dispensationalism thus confirms that Christianity began not in the Holy Land in the meridian of time but with Adam in the very beginning. Hence, instead of wondering why similar fragments and shards of truth appear in various and disparate cultures, some of these parallels actually result from original wholeness and subsequent shatterings and scatterings.

"Undoubtedly the knowledge of this law and of other rites and ceremonies was carried by the posterity of Adam into all lands, and continued with them, more or less pure, to the flood, and through Noah, who was a 'preacher of righteousness,' to those who succeeded him, spreading out in all nations and countries, Adam and Noah being the first of their dispensations to receive them from God. What wonder, then, that we should find relics of Christianity so to speak among the heathens, and nations who know not Christ, and whose histories date back beyond the days of Moses, and even beyond the flood, independent of and apart from the records of the Bible."[9]

Thus, the Restoration, through its revelations and translations, has brought back many—not just a few—"plain and precious things," things once "taken away" or "kept back" (1 Nephi 13:28–29, 32, 34, 40). The truths, especially those underscoring the divinity of Jesus Christ, are happily "had again" (Moses 1:41).

People who have only "the lesser portion of the word" (Alma 12:10)—often through no fault of their own—lack a fulness of understanding of Jesus. In our secular time, many deny spiritual things, forgetting that "to be learned is good" only if that learning does not diminish our hearkening to the "counsels of God" (2 Nephi 9:29). In such a spiritual vacuum, people naturally "preach up unto themselves their own wisdom and their own learning," featuring the "world and the wisdom thereof" (2 Nephi 26:20; 1 Nephi 11:35). In their pride and vain imaginations, they unfortunately and insistently "put down the power of God" (2 Nephi 26:20; see also 1 Nephi 12:18).

This lengthy period in human history of doctrinal deprivation because of a loss of many "plain and precious things" (1 Nephi 13:28) was foretold to Moses anciently:

"And now, Moses, my son, I will speak unto thee concerning this earth upon which thou standest; and thou shalt write the things which I shall speak.

"And in a day when the children of men shall esteem my words as naught and take many of them from the book which thou shalt write, behold, I will raise up another like unto thee; and they shall be had again among the children of men—among as many as shall believe" (Moses 1:40–41).

The things lost include the "plain and most precious" and the "most plain" (1 Nephi 13:26, 34). These things—whether "taken away" or "kept back"—do not appear fully in the precious Holy Bible (1 Nephi 13:26, 32). For such things to be "had again" through the Restoration "in word, and also in power" is truly a very special thing (Moses 1:41; 1 Nephi 14:1). When we encounter it, our emotions often exceed our understanding of it. Inspired poets can help.

Consider these poetic words from Henry Vaughan (1622–1695) which are germane to what Latter-day Saints call premortality, that vital doctrine laid out so helpfully in the Restoration.

THE RETREAT

Happy those early days, when I
shined in my Angel-infancy!
Before I understood this place
Appointed for my second race,
Or taught my soul to fancy aught
But a white, celestial thought;
When yet I had not walked above
A mile or two from my first Love,
And looking back, at that short space
Could see a glimpse of His bright face;
When on some gilded cloud or flower
My gazing soul would dwell an hour,
And in those weaker glories spy
Some shadows of eternity.[10]

Why should we be surprised when, yearning and believing, others approximate what for us has come as revealed knowledge? Indeed, "God is mindful of every people, whatsoever land they may be in; yea, he numbereth his

28

people, and his bowels of mercy are over all the earth" (Alma 26:37).

Alexander Pope spoke of the marvels of this universe of which man is a part. He described it as "a mighty maze! but not without a plan." He wrote of "worlds unnumber'd tho' the God be known" and how it is "ours to trace him only in our own." Pope likewise wrote of how "other planets circle other suns."[11] All these bring to mind certain restoration scriptures about how all the worlds cannot be numbered unto man but are numbered unto God (Moses 1:37).

We do not worship a one-planet God! The Lord told Moses, "But only an account of this earth, and the inhabitants thereof, give I unto you" (Moses 1:35). Even so, the Lord has told us some soaring things: "That by [Christ] the worlds are and were created, and the inhabitants thereof are begotten sons and daughters unto God" (D&C 76:24).

This earth was formed to be inhabited (Isaiah 45:18). Why? "For behold, this is my work and my glory—to bring to pass the immortality and eternal life of man" (Moses 1:39). Stephen Hawking, displaying that meekness which is found in great scientists, wrote: "Although science may solve the problem of how the universe began, it cannot answer the question: Why does the universe bother to exist? I don't know the answer to that."[12]

We are deservedly excited by the periodic space probes which can help us to know more about the what and the how. But the more we know about them, the more haunting the "why?" questions become. The answers to the "why" questions are actually obtainable only by the revelations given by our creating God.

The Lord has created "worlds without number" to achieve His announced purposes (Moses 1:33, 39). Unsurprisingly, the theology of the Restoration is not tied to any particular or developing theories of astrophysics, but its relevant revelations are expansive and give us a few inklings. Meanwhile, able scientists press forward.

For instance, some astronomers say they have discovered an "enormous wall . . . of galaxies . . . the largest structure yet observed in the universe."[13] These scientists say of the recent discoveries, "We keep seeing something bigger as we go out farther."[14] Latter-day Saints should not be surprised, however, because the Lord has said there is "no end to my works" (Moses 1:38).

There is pattern and order in the universe. Kolob, for example, "standeth above the earth" but "belong[eth] to the same order," Abraham was told, "as the [planet] upon which thou standest" (Abraham 3:5, 1). Scientists say these nonrandom "galaxies appear to be arranged in a network of strings, or filaments, surrounding large, relatively empty regions of space known as voids."[15]

Furthermore, our own "galaxy, the Milky Way, is located in one of the relatively empty spaces between the Great Walls."[16] Significantly, the Lord told Abraham, "There is space there, . . . and we will make an earth" (Abraham 3:24).

One eminent scientist is quoted as saying, "As we look out into the Universe and identify the many accidents of physics and astronomy that have worked together to our benefit, it almost seems as if the Universe must in some sense have known that we were coming."[17]

The Lord's work, as revelations advise us, is thus very, very large! "The heavens declare the glory of God; and the firmament sheweth his handywork" (Psalm 19:1). Amid this vastness, Enoch, as noted, affirmed of God, "Yet thou art there" (Moses 7:30). The multiplicity of God's creations interested Enoch less than the personalness and redemptiveness of God!

Occasionally, when Church members testify of and focus on the Restoration and its implications, doing so can make others uncomfortable and a few even resentful. Do we do it to be unfriendly? Of course not. Or, in order to seem to be "one up"? We certainly should not. In so testifying, it may appear to some that we are not sufficiently accommodating in achieving a larger peer harmony. Do we proceed anyway? Yes—but meekly.

Given the profound implications of the Restoration, we really have no choice. Even so, genuine love and meekness are crucial in sharing the good news, and bearers of such good tidings are sometimes poorly received. Yet, we are divinely directed to share the "good news" of the gospel with mankind—the message is, after all, not merely about a temporary bargain at a nearby supermarket! Consider the "good news": God and some of His angels have actually visited the earth! Revelations have come regarding the true identity of mortals and the purposes and meaning of human life! The same Restoration has brought forth additional holy scriptures to company with the precious Holy Bible! Likewise called anew are apostles and prophets, ancient callings so much needed in our time! Similarly, many holy temples are being brought forth on a sizable scale, each offering the ordinances necessary for mortals to go Home to our Father God!

A sense of proportion is therefore vital as to communicating with peers. In World War I, the British were deeply concerned with the consequences of savage submarine warfare. Urgently, an antisubmarine committee had been formed on which the eminent British physicist, Ernest Rutherford, served. Rutherford missed a meeting of experts advising the British government on antisubmarine warfare. When criticized, he replied: "I have been engaged in experiments which

31

suggest that the atom can be artificially disintegrated. If it is true, it is of far greater importance than a war."[18]

Meek Church members will freely acknowledge that the circumstances of our taking the gospel to the world are ironical in some respects. We are still a small and obscure people, though chosen to serve in "a marvelous work and a wonder" (2 Nephi 25:17). Ancient Israel was reminded by the Lord, however, "The Lord did not set his love upon you, nor choose you, because ye were more in number than any people; for ye were the fewest of all people" (Deuteronomy 7:7).

The same comparative obscurity attaches to our planet Earth, which is really a speck of sand in the suburbs of the Milky Way galaxy, one of thousands of galaxies. Similarly, a tiny stretch of sand hosted Jesus' meridian ministry, so minuscule in terms of geography.

In view of the "good news," we certainly need to be meek. But can we really be silent? Others are clearly free to reject this good news, and we need to be ever courteous and sensitive in sharing. But we do not have the luxury of being mute concerning "a marvelous work and a wonder" by muffling the message of the Restoration.

Consider how President Gordon B. Hinckley has undertaken so many extra efforts to build bridges with others, counseling us to be more careful and thoughtful than we sometimes are with regard to others:

"We can all be a little kinder, a little more generous, a little more thoughtful of one another. We can be a little more tolerant and friendly to those not of our faith, going out of our way to show our respect for them. We cannot afford to be arrogant or self-righteous. It is our obligation to reach out in helpfulness not only to our own but to all others as well."[19]

Yet President Hinckley has also been boldly declarative, saying:

"We stand on the summit of the ages, awed by a great and solemn sense of history. This is the last and final dispensation toward which all in the past has pointed. I bear testimony and witness of the reality and truth of these things."[20]

Therefore, when others reject our efforts to share, their rejection or indifference should not limit our generosity, courtesy, or civility toward them.

Of course, if the work of the Restoration were merely the work of men, it would come to naught along with so many other causes marginal in their effects. Instead, we are dealing with the work of God and with His assurance that He can surely and certainly bring His purposes to pass. God's determinations, therefore, provide the vaulting reassurance that we all need as we proceed along the demanding path of discipleship, and His long-suffering provides balm for the footsore.

3

DIVINE DETERMINATION

Given the times of commotion but being bolstered by the countervailing steadiness and nourishing richness of the Restoration, it becomes imperative for us to have faith in God and in His capacity to bring His purposes to pass—He, in fact, has made "ample provision" to achieve that glorious outcome![1] Such a God with perfect capacities and sublime purposes does more than just exist. Even with faith in a personal, perfect, and proactive God, however, we will be tested. Moreover, on occasions, we have witnessed and will witness human suffering so poignant that we need to be reassured.

Some disciples do seem to face a simultaneous multiplicity of challenges. Some have tests that they must live with protractedly, while others are passing through an intense "small moment" (D&C 121:7). Those individuals in live-with situations would gladly give "more praise for relief," but it does not always come in this life.[2] Their constellation of challenges seems unending as well as rending. To these enduring individuals, surely the prepositional phrase "to the end" has a special meaning; their so doing represents a very commendable and special achievement (Matthew 10:22; 1 Nephi 13:37; D&C 14:7; 121:8).

The rest of us are in admiration, even awe, of them. Understandably, in the midst of their enduring faithfulness, such meek individuals may at times ponder and puzzle over their own faith or worthiness. Yet if we examine these words, "Nevertheless the Lord seeth fit to chasten his people; yea, he trieth their patience and their faith," we see how faith and patience can be tried and thereby deliberately developed (Mosiah 23:21). Faith and patience provide a special and combined power—whether it is a live-with or pass-through circumstance or whether it is one thing or a demanding combination of things. One outcome of chastening of whatever form can be "to purify." Relief may come, but only after the trial of faith and patience (Ether 12:6).

Our own suffering seems small compared to what these noble individuals live with. As we all know, Jesus reminded a genuinely suffering Joseph Smith that he was "not yet as Job" (D&C 121:10). Only Jesus can compare crosses! (Alma 7:11–12). Nevertheless, we can admire, love, emulate, and pray for those who endure well, because special individuals are examples for us all.

When they cope successfully, we inwardly applaud them and gladly certify to their emerging character. Though admiring, however, the rest of us tremble at the tuition required for the shaping and polishing of such sterling character. Furthermore, we hope we would not falter should similar circumstances come to us!

When witnessing in others the relentlessness and the protractedness or the suffering in this personal process, one recalls the lengthy, stretching, and collective travails in Sinai before Israel finally entered the promised land. The land of eventual exit was clearly promised, but, meanwhile, there were all the disappointing daily destinations and desolate way stations which marked the discouraging zigzag pattern.

More frequently, of course, when we see others being polished, it is much less dramatic. It involves, instead, the smoothing sandpaper of daily circumstances, but the same determined, divine redemptiveness is at work amid the routine rubbings of life.

In either situation, the object is for our wills to be finally "swallowed up in the will of the Father" (Mosiah 15:7), eventually bringing to us the joys gladly given by the Father and constituting "all that He hath" (Genesis 24:36). In a very real sense, therefore, what we can take now foretells what He can give later! This reality should be kept firmly in mind as we understandably pray for relief from short-term stress or long-term trauma. We would, if we could, put periods, if not exclamation points, where God is content to put commas in the process.

Either way, the "process of time" is needed to facilitate our incremental improvement (Moses 7:21). Therein, individual increments of personal improvement are often scarcely discernable by themselves, yet the cumulative process moves us ever closer to Home.

Successfully traversed, the individual Sinais of stretching can facilitate our developing and better emulating Christ's attributes. Along with receiving His ordinances and keeping our covenants with Him, each of these attributes also certifies our eventual admissibility to the celestial kingdom.

Hence, the stretching trek requires deep faith in God's existence, deep faith in God's purposes, and also deep faith in His timing. The latter is sometimes most difficult to develop, yet "the cross comes before the crown."[3]

As a true and perfect Father, He desires that each of His children develop righteously and fully. Furthermore, He will not always and automatically intervene to block every stressful and needful experience. His withholding occurs because He loves us determinedly. In fact, we know enough about God's plan of salvation to realize that His perfect love and His desire for our happiness are truly inestimable—so much so that He permits us to pass through certain experiences, even if these might momentarily stagger the soul. Think of Abraham and Isaac! (Genesis 22:1–14). Abraham's previous history was a preparatory one in which he "staggered not" at supernal promises (Romans 4:20). Think especially of divine determination displayed by both the Father and the Son at Gethsemane and Calvary!

Hard to bear, too, is the reality that the harsh consequences and human suffering arising from sin and iniquity are not confined to the causal evildoers themselves. The resulting human suffering brought by wars, famines, and awful genocides can tax our faith, too, as we see the ooze of suffering spread so widely from the point of initiation.

Yet God's commitment to mankind's moral agency is very deep. Moreover, man's choices do have consequences! Never mind that some mortals foolishly think they have both the freedom to choose and the freedom from any adverse consequences. So it is that family, neighbors, and friends so often suffer innocently from the toxic waste of another's sins—be these a betraying husband and father, a mother enticed from the nest, rebellious offspring, or the lust for riches, power, and dominance.

Given the earnestness with which God pursues His divine tutoring, it is comforting to know that we worship a God who on occasion weeps—and Enoch saw Him weep! (Moses 7:27–29). Yet we also worship a God who has made "ample provision" amid human wickedness to bring all His purposes to pass.[4] Still, observing the process in its near extremes on occasion causes the soul to shiver.

Our faith in God must be strong, therefore, not only in behalf of ourselves and our own trials but also upon seeing those human conditions involving human wickedness which are truly wrenching but which are permitted because of God-given but mortally misused agency.

The havoc and debris of misused agency are at times appalling. The slums wrought by iniquity and the junkyards left by juvenescent behavior dot the landscape. Why does not God put a stop to it and clean them up? Because agency is so central to His plan of happiness! Our best and highest perorations and mortal expressions concerning the value of freedom and liberty must seem so callow, though sincere, compared to God's reasons for our having agency.

Even when we make some spiritual progress, we need further help in order to face yet another discomfiting reality: our appreciated blessings should not obscure the developmental distance yet to be traveled. The need for this added meekness was noted by C. S. Lewis:

"Little people like you and me, if our prayers are sometimes granted, beyond all hope and probability, had better not draw hasty conclusions to our own advantage. If we were stronger, we might be less tenderly treated. If we were braver, we might be sent, with far less help, to defend far more desperate posts in the great battle."[5]

Even so, the Master Mentor has comfortingly promised, "I will lead you along" (D&C 78:18). He has also said, "Ye cannot bear all things now" (D&C 78:18). Ponder, however, the implications of the word *now*. Precisely because He loves us, on occasion there may need to be a further ratcheting up in the degree of difficulty in our discipleship.

The following words, unarguably declarative, about

divine determination are both reassuring and wintry: "There is nothing that the Lord thy God shall take in his heart to do but what he will do it" (Abraham 3:17). After all, the premortal declaration of divine intent concerning what lay ahead for God's spirit children was the sobering "[Let us] prove them herewith" (Abraham 3:25).

Even if and when we seem to have squeezed out the last full measure of our devotion, an omniscient and perfectly empathic God not only knows the difficulties through which we have passed and are passing but also knows if any residue of unused devotion still remains to further the process! (Alma 7:11–12).

He knows, too, what joy awaits us, if we are fully submissive. In fact, we are even counseled concerning our appreciative mortal exclamations over beauty: "Eye hath not seen, nor ear heard, neither have entered into the heart of man, the things which God hath prepared for them that love him" (1 Corinthians 2:9). It is a caution which also invites anticipation. Meanwhile, we can become much better prepared for joy *then* by increasing our capacity *now*. Hence, some anticipatory tingling is permissible, but a sobering willingness to be stretched is also required. Much more than heightening our appreciation is involved. Besides, divine justice and mercy finally ensure that each of us will receive "according to [our] wills" and desires (Alma 29:4). How could any later complain?

Meanwhile, divine determination also insists that we will not experience a shortage of the needed clinical experiences (Abraham 3:25; Mosiah 23:21). For instance, when the Lord notes, in effect, "one thing thou lackest," we will not likely want for the clinical experiences necessary to remedy any such deficiency (Mark 10:21; Luke 18:22). No wonder it is so vital for us to understand both the character and the purposes of our God as mirrored in His divine determination.

"If a man learns nothing more than to eat, drink and sleep, and does not comprehend any of the designs of God, the beast comprehends the same things. It eats, drinks, sleeps, and knows nothing more about God; yet it knows as much as we, unless we are able to comprehend by the inspiration of Almighty God. If men do not comprehend the character of God, they do not comprehend themselves."[6]

Besides, there is nothing through which we will pass, including sicknesses, pain, and grief, that Jesus has not experienced personally (Alma 7:11–12). He knows our varying capacities. Just as important, He proffers grace and help—out of His matchless empathy (Ether 12:27).

Moreover, in even the deepest of our prayers, it is not as though we are telling God something about our sufferings or concerns that He does not already personally know (Matthew 6:32; Alma 7:11–12). More than once, through His prophets, He reminds us that He comprehends everything, though clearly we do not (Mosiah 4:9; 2 Nephi 2:24; 9:20; Alma 26:35; D&C 38:2).

Still, some finite mortals ironically insist on a more indulgent God with whom they are much more comfortable!

"For if God is a socially conscious political being whose views invariably correspond to our own prejudices on every essential point of doctrine, he demands of us no more than our politics require. Besides, if God is finite, progressive, and Pure Love, we may as well skip church next Sunday and go to the movies. For if we have nothing to fear from this all-loving, all-forbearing, all-forgiving God, how would our worship of him constitute more than self-congratulation for our own moral standards? As an atheist, *I like this God. It is good to see him every morning while I am shaving.*"[7]

Actually, to deny the attributes of God, such as His determination and empathy, is to deny His Godhood, especially His love:

"Now my brethren, we see that God is mindful of every people, whatsoever land they may be in; yea, he numbereth his people, and his bowels of mercy are over all the earth. Now this is my joy, and my great thanksgiving; yea, and I will give thanks unto my God forever. Amen" (Alma 26:37).

Comparatively, we cannot even empathize fully with—let alone love perfectly—all in our own families or in our tiny neighborhoods! It is partly so because the needed developmental process will not really proceed until the natural man begins to be put off by us (Mosiah 3:19). The encrusted natural man simply stays on square one and does not even seek to comprehend. For this there is a fundamental cause:

"And now behold, my brethren, what natural man is there that knoweth these things? I say unto you, there is none that knoweth these things, save it be the penitent" (Alma 26:21).

Yes, the unfashionable virtue of penitence is a prelude to learning the things of God!

Being penitent, however, is not natural to the natural man. Therefore, our task of putting off the natural man is urgent in order to facilitate our continuing education! (Mosiah 3:19).

Thus, fatally flawed because he thinks so highly only of himself, the natural man has no room left in his narrow life to worship an all-loving and all-comprehending God or to serve his neighbor. In the earthly focus of his desires, the natural man refuses to pay the costs of exaltation; he is too comfortable playing in castled sand piles and living in second-class hotels. Mansions are beyond his ken.

At first, the declaration "the natural man is an enemy of

God" may seem to be harsh. Let us remember, however, who declared and whose minions wage against God's plan of happiness (Mosiah 3:19).

Often unconscious of being mired in misery, the natural man insists on remaining as he is, undisturbed. Repeatedly, he refuses to consider what he has the power to become (Alma 26:4). Instead, the natural man manages to get his ticket punched at almost every stop on the temptation train; after all, it seems so natural. Being unpenitent, he regards the similar behavior of other passengers merely as confirmation of his own conclusion: "I am only human" (see Alma 26:21). Moreover, if he is sorry at all, it is not "godly sorrow" he feels (2 Corinthians 7:10); rather, he is sorry for the inconvenience of his being discovered or interrupted.

As Jesus said, some "justify [themselves] before men; for that which is . . . an abomination before God" (Luke 16:15). Instead of pursuing his repentance, the natural man's shoulder-shrugging self-indulgence demands our forgiveness (2 Corinthians 7:10). Sensuality thus has its own form of assertive self-pity!

Sending words his way may not help the natural man, because, as Jesus said, "Lusts . . . choke the word" (Mark 4:19). Effectively, the natural man is already "shut out from the presence of God" (Moses 6:49).

So the natural man insists on being the pseudo orphan— he either does not hear or refuses the loving calls to come to his real Home! Even if perchance he should hear the voice of God, it will be regarded only as brief and interrupting thunder in the distance (John 12:29). The distraction passes; hence, so he can hurry back to the sand piles!

Our minds—and with them, desires—have to be changed. Our minds, according to the Prophet Joseph Smith, represent such a special portion of us, something which is eternal:

"I take my ring from my finger and liken it unto the mind of man—the immortal part, because it has no beginning. . . . So with the spirit of man."[8]

In fact, our minds can become much more like the "mind of Christ" (1 Corinthians 2:16). The same apostle worried, for instance, that we might "faint in [our] minds" or become "shaken in mind" (Hebrews 12:3; 2 Thessalonians 2:2). One remedy is for us to be "renewed in the spirit of [our] mind[s]" (Ephesians 4:23). In this dispensation, too, the Lord has emphasized that we "not be weary in mind" (D&C 84:80).

A promise was given by God anciently to His covenant people that He would "put [His] laws into their mind" (Hebrews 8:10). Does this somehow account for the spiritual resonance we sometimes feel and see? Or, does this tell us why the words of the Lord have a "more powerful effect upon the minds of the people" than anything else? (Alma 31:5). A meek mind responds to the doctrines of the Lord, because "my sheep hear my voice" (John 10:27).

When the mind is not firm, however, a range of reactions is seen: an individual can either be insistently indifferent or may instead be wrought up "by the great tribulations of his mind" (Alma 15:3). This latter condition relates to the Prophet Joseph Smith's observations about the special trial that "suspense" can constitute, observing that "there is no pain so awful as the pain of suspense."[9] The Prophet was using the word *suspense* in the context of how knowledge does away with darkness, suspense, and doubt. A lack of knowledge is one of the condemnations of the wicked, their hell being their unknowingness about such matters as their identities, destinies, and possibilities.

Since the Lord has told us that His ways are higher than man's ways, therefore, the process of repentance begins in our mind. It is a process which causes us to change our mind to reflect better the mind of Christ.[10] If we are meek instead of bitter, our capacity for empathy, for example, is to a great extent rooted in our experiences and memories.

"[But trials] will only give us that knowledge to understand the minds of the Ancients. For my part I think I never could have felt as I now do if I had not suffered the wrongs that I have suffered. All things shall work together for good to them that love God."[11]

Thus, we are encouraged to have a "willing mind" (D&C 64:34). The ultimate submissiveness is when our "minds become single" and submissive to God by being "swallowed up in [His] will" (Mosiah 15:7; D&C 88:68). Clearly excluded is the adversary who "knew not the mind of God" (Moses 4:6).

Of necessity, since agency reigns, Paul and all the prophets want people to "be fully persuaded in [their] own mind[s]" (Romans 14:5). However enticing the shortcuts may seem, to persuade one against his will only requires more arduous backpacking and backtracking!

How vital that our minds feast upon the words of Christ and that we be firm and unshaken as we encounter the challenges of life! Thus, if meek, our minds understandably reach out with regard to God: Is He really there? Enoch was mightily reassured! (Moses 7:30). Does God know me? Perfectly! Does He love me? Perfectly! Does He really have particularized plans for me? Indeed! Such fundamental feelings and wonderments are responded to fully, as we come to know better the character, purposes, and the capacity of God.

To do His redemptive work daily thus requires understanding His doctrines and having them constantly refreshed and renewed, lest we "faint" in our minds or become "weary" in mind (Hebrews 12:3; D&C 84:80). Peter used the metaphor which urges us to "gird up the loins of your mind" (1 Peter 1:13). Therefore, a one-time, intellectual acceptance of doctrines to then be filed away is simply not enough. In discipleship there must be interactiveness of intellect and behavior.

There must likewise be a constancy in the nourishment of the mind by truth and by "having your loins girt about with truth" (Ephesians 6:14; D&C 27:16). The dictionary defines *gird* as to bind, to make fast, to surround, and to prepare for action, suggesting anything but isolation, intellectual flabbiness, or lassitude. Our own capacity to gird up must grow if we are to emulate divine determination on our own scale of discipleship. After all, is not discipleship grounded in discipline? Faltering as we sometimes are, we are blessed to worship a loving Father God who mercifully is perfect in His long-suffering.

4

THE LONG-SUFFERING LORD

Our personal long-suffering, when expressed by mortals towards others, includes our experiencing and enduring the shortfalls caused by errant mortals. Because of our own and their repeated misuse of agency, there is certainly adequate clinical material available to practice our long-suffering on. Widespread misuse of human agency causes so much injury, trouble, distress, anxiety, and needless provocation in human relationships. Vital though long-suffering is, however, most of us are not yet very practiced in extending this important virtue toward others—or in reducing our own erroneous ways which require extending the virtue to us.

Contrastingly, divine long-suffering, of course, is perfect. Moreover, we all need it not only in our own behalf but also for providing us with a beckoning Model. Yet the Perfect Bestower of long-suffering is not without tears of His own (Moses 7).

Of the need for us to develop this quality, the Prophet Joseph said, "The nearer we get to our heavenly Father, the more we are disposed to look with compassion on perishing souls."[1] The Prophet, who "learned by sad experience" (D&C 121:39), received many criticisms, some of which reflected sad shortfalls in the understanding of others toward him:

"'O, if I were Brother Joseph I would do this and that'; but if they were in Brother Joseph's shoes they would find that men or women could not be compelled into the kingdom of God, but must be dealt with in long-suffering."[2]

Happily, the Lord exemplifies for us perfect long-suffering. Paul wrote of how Jesus Christ shows "forth all long-suffering, for a pattern to them which should hereafter believe on him" (1 Timothy 1:16). The Lord's long-suffering is perfect; He is full of love, mercy, and goodness, and His "charity suffereth long" (1 Corinthians 13:4; Exodus 34:6). As ever, it remains for us to be more emulative of Him.

In so many ways, not only do we rely upon the application of the divine qualities all the time but just knowing of their reality and the possibility of some attainment of these by us gives genuine hope. No wonder we are to let the long-suffering of the Lord "rest in [our] mind[s] forever" (Moroni 9:25).

Peter, for instance, described how, in a previous time of major social deterioration, the long-suffering of the Lord "waited in the days of Noah" (1 Peter 3:20). Like the Noachians, our society, aware or not, is very dependent upon the Lord's divine patience and long-suffering. Mercifully for us all, He is "not willing that any should perish," a divine posture absolutely essential for us in order to "work out [our] salvation" (2 Peter 3:9; Alma 34:37). In between the mortal misuse of our agency and the justice of God, the lubricant of His long-suffering is much needed. Not to be confused with mortal indulgence, His long-suffering recognizes and facilitates what can happen in us developmentally "in process of time" (Moses 7:21).

The acting out of our errant desires, however, ensures needless human suffering. Our lack of selfish impulse control so often ends up abusing others. Our short fuses are in such stark contrast to God's long-suffering!

Unsurprisingly, those who become aware of how they themselves are blessed beneficiaries of divine long-suffering are much more likely, in turn, to be benefactors of other mortals in need of long-suffering. Praise be to those who so proffer and persist in such patience! Hence, our long-suffering involves more than an intellectual awareness of what is amiss. The anxious father of the prodigal son was much more than a detached desk clerk waiting to see who would check in.

The scripturally prescribed pattern for acting with such redemptiveness of attitude includes both long-suffering and doctrine. Since our God is the God of truth, His doctrines, when understood, provide a firm and substantive basis for using "persuasion" and all "long-suffering," because there is something solid to be persuaded about (D&C 121:41). Knowledge of doctrines, therefore, can provide a vital focus for our otherwise diffused feelings (2 Corinthians 6:6). Interwoven with divine doctrines are knowable, divine standards designed to prevent us from drifting toward mere indulgence. Nothing is quite so sad as being sorry but without any real or redeeming standards. Yet we see it all the time.

For example, it is instructive and inspirational as to the Lord's long-suffering for us to know that the original Twelve, once gently chided by Jesus for being unable to wait a mere hour (Matthew 26:40), will nevertheless one day stand "at [Jesus'] right hand at the day of [His] coming in a pillar of fire, being clothed with robes of righteousness, with crowns upon their heads, in glory even as [He is], to judge the whole house of Israel" (D&C 29:12). Divine long-suffering gives genuine hope and can bring later specific blessings to all who now falter and fall short from time to time.

Yet God's mentoring accompanies his long-suffering. As the brother of Jared exemplified, painful reproof may precede generous praise (Ether 2:14; 3:9). Hence, God's long-suffering is not indulgence. Though He does not want any to perish, His redemptive process nevertheless requires that all should come unto repentance, a stern and specific process (Mosiah 28:3; D&C 18:44). Thereby, however, we may achieve genuine reconciliation with Him and submission to Him.

Families, leaders, friends, and neighbors can help this process, especially if we "preach the word; [are] instant in season, out of season; reprove, rebuke, exhort with all long-suffering and doctrine" (2 Timothy 4:2). We can also best assist if, first of all, we, ourselves "have come to a knowledge of the goodness of God, and his matchless power, and his wisdom, and his patience, and his long-suffering towards the children of men; and also, the atonement which has been prepared from the foundation of the world" (Mosiah 4:6).

The first verse in the Book of Mormon, best known for its praise of parents, also includes Nephi's testimony of his learning and knowing of the "goodness" of God (1 Nephi 1:1). More than we sometimes do, we, too, should testify to the reality of God but also to the blessed reality of His character, as did Nephi. Nurturing and coping parents can show the way, as did Lehi and Sariah.

The more we strive to express long-suffering toward others, the greater and deeper our adoration of the Lord will become, reflecting ever greater appreciation for this perfect quality in Him.

Given our moral agency, God's long-suffering becomes vitally necessary for God to tutor us in process of time, encouraging the further alignment of our own desires with His. Even if such aligning finally fails to happen fully, God's mercy and loving kindness and long-suffering will nevertheless have striven with us, and the record will be clear. God's many specific entreaties will have been rejected because of our rebelliousness. Even though His redemptive arm was "lengthened out all the day long" (2 Nephi 28:32), it is often unnoticed, or turned aside, by many who could have grasped it.

In addition to our mistaking God's long-suffering for indulgence, there is another error we can make. For example, we can wrongly conclude there is no real hurry for us to change. Contemporary society is awash in these two errors. Thereby, needed opportunities for our repentance pass unused, creating real casualties and victims. Thereby, too, estrangement from Jesus is further widened by the dulling of our capacity for genuine spiritual sensitivity or even redeeming shame. Shame is an emotion to which some moderns have become almost total strangers (Mosiah 5:13). No vertigo is as vicious as in those who try to "spin" their shame! Shame is so much more than a face made briefly warm and red. Real shame scalds the soul.

Thus, frail and imperfect as we may be now, the failure to develop the divine attributes, including long-suffering and justice, does create real victims in marriages, at work, among families, friends, and neighbors.

Consider, for instance, the awful perils of a political system which is significantly estranged from truth—whether in dialogue, in the public record, or in campaigns. Being politically offended but without spiritual standards is not the same thing as righteous indignation.

Likewise, ponder how the absence of graciousness in human relationships automatically exalts rudeness, bringing so much brittleness in human interactions and communications.

Vengeance is directly opposite to long-suffering. "Getting even" does not really balance the scales at all; it only distorts them even further—whether practiced between nations, tribes, or spouses!

Perhaps most sobering, when compared to genuine long-suffering of Him who is perfect in His love, is the impatient, mortal misuse of power, which carries such awful consequences. In *Notes from the House of the Dead,* Fyodor Dostoyevsky wrote of grossly misused power:

"Whoever has experienced the power, the complete ability to humiliate another human being . . . with the most extreme humiliation, willy-nilly loses power over his own sensations. Tyranny is a habit, it has a capacity for development, it develops finally into a disease. . . . The human being and the citizen die within the tyrant forever; return to humanity, to repentance, to regeneration becomes almost impossible."[3]

There are those—more than a few—who really do have an actual lust to govern or to boss others. One sees it in small businesses as well as in big governments. Historian Barbara Tuchman wrote insightfully:

"Chief among the forces affecting political folly is lust for power, named by Tacitus, as 'the most flagrant of all the passions.' Because it can only be satisfied by power over others, government is its favorite field of exercise."[4]

Our experiences with power can help us to appreciate better how God's power reflects His perfect love, accompanied by mercy and long-suffering. On a mortal scale, one learns of it in President George Washington: "In all history few men who possessed unassailable power have used that power so gently and self-effacingly for what their best instincts told them was the welfare of their neighbors and all mankind."[5]

Mortals have not yet invented a pride meter which would be the equivalent of the wristbands or other warning devices worn by workers in nuclear facilities. The latter can detect and show when the level of radioactivity has reached dangerous levels. We do not have a counterpart that warns us of the deadly surges of gross, prideful arrogance, which can take an even more devastating toll.

Our present capacity for meekness is doubtless reflective of how much we had already developed that quality in the premortal world. Its further development can be greatly enhanced by family life, discipleship, and so on. Furthermore, the disparities in meekness among mortals are too great to attribute solely to the mortal environment; we brought certain "luggage" with us.

As we strive to emulate Jesus, it is reassuring for us to know that the Prophet Joseph Smith spoke of how true disciples can eventually reach the point where they lose all desire for sin—and this would include the desire to compel and dominate others. But, he observed realistically, "This is a station to which no man ever arrived in a moment."[6] Developmental discipleship is thus incremental, another self-evident reason for us to rejoice in the long-suffering of the Lord and to ponder anew the need for that attribute and patience in ourselves.

The Lord's higher ways can become our ways (Isaiah 55:9). But if the disparity between ours and the Lord's ways is too great, too obvious, and too frequent, others may actually be turned away from His gospel and Church. Sadly, at one time the pride of Church members was greater than that of those who did not belong to the Church (Alma 4:9–10).

Therefore, may people experience us as genuinely striving to become more and more like the Lord we worship. After all, we are each other's clinical material. Given that reality, there is this sobering reminder from President Brigham Young about the need for patience:

"There are no two faces alike, no two persons tempered alike; . . . we are tried with each other, and large drafts are made upon our patience, forbearance, charity, and good will—in short, upon all the higher and godlike qualities of our nature."[7]

Even given the foregoing descriptions of the need for long-suffering, are there moments when, out of love, we should "admonish . . . sharply" or reprove "with sharpness"? (D&C 112:12; 121:43). Of course! But as Paul cautions, we should do so in such a way that the reproved are not "swallowed up with overmuch sorrow" (2 Corinthians 2:7). Nor should we proceed further than the healing balm within us, as Brigham Young counseled the Saints:

"If you are ever called upon to chasten a person, never chasten beyond the balm you have within you to bind up. . . . I say again, Do not chasten beyond the balm you have within you. . . . When you have the chastening rod in your hands, ask God to give you wisdom to use it, that you may not use it to the destruction of an individual, but to his salvation."[8]

We especially need more long-suffering when "large drafts are made upon our patience." President Young spoke on the degrees of chastisement:

"True, there are degrees of feeling and degrees of chastisement, and you are led to chastise one man differently to what you do another. You may, figuratively speaking, pound one Elder over the head with a club, and he does not know but what you have handed him a straw dipped in molasses to suck. There are others, if you speak a word to them, or take up a straw and chasten them, whose hearts are broken; they are as tender in their feelings as an infant, and will melt like wax before the flame. You must not chasten them severely; you must chasten according to the spirit that is in the person. Some you may talk to all day long, and they do not know what you are talking about. There is a great variety. Treat people as they are."[9]

If Jesus can plead to a perfectly merciful Father, why should we not emulate Him by having greater long-suffering but also by genuinely pleading in behalf of others? (D&C 45:3–4). Then our souls can be further enlarged and "without hypocrisy" (D&C 121:42). Then, "without compulsory means," certain blessings will flow to us forever (D&C 121:46).

Again to be emphasized is that long-suffering can still be discerning (1 Chronicles 28:9; Alma 18:32). The prophet Mormon soon came to discern a crucial distinction in his contemporaries, as we may, too:

"When I, Mormon, saw their lamentation and their mourning and their sorrow before the Lord, my heart did begin to rejoice within me, knowing the mercies and the long-suffering of the Lord, therefore supposing that he would be merciful unto them that they would again become a righteous people.

"But behold this my joy was vain, for their sorrowing was not unto repentance, because of the goodness of God; but it was rather the sorrowing of the damned, because the Lord would not always suffer them to take happiness in sin" (Mormon 2:12–13).

Still, some may continue to think mistakenly that a long-suffering God is a soft touch. A soft touch, like the tutoring trail of tears in Sinai or in handcart country? A soft touch, given the determined tutoring described in "all these things shall give thee experience, and shall be for thy good"? (D&C 122:7). A soft touch, like the Father's silence in response to deserving Jesus' plea in Gethsemane that the cup be taken from him and the earlier "Father, save me from this hour"? (John 12:27; Matthew 26:39).

No wonder, therefore, the "word" may need to be sharp at times so "it cutteth them to the very center" (1 Nephi 16:2). A softening of hearts sometimes requires more than a soft touch.

If our wills are submissively tied to God's will, only then is His yoke really easier to bear (Matthew 11:29–30). Unless our inner desires are becoming more and more like His, His yoke will chafe and torture our shoulders. To boast "I can handle it," without any inner meekness, is to set up oneself for failure. The adversary doubtless notes any superficial boasts by women and men alike.

Because He was and is so perfectly meek and lowly, Jesus submitted His will to the Father's will. For us, truly doing likewise may seem so out of reach, partly because we ironically insist on attaching hindering conditions to our submission. There is so much hesitance and holding back.

For some, the process of time can help, as it did for the prodigal son, in order to come to themselves (Luke 15:17). Necessary, too, was the patience and long-suffering of the father of the prodigal. We are not told of his earlier and anguished waiting . . . and waiting. How oft did his anxious eyes scan the horizon?

If we exercise more long-suffering toward others, doing so reflects not only an increased love but a quality of love which refuses to give up. In effect, it is like saying to the errant one, "I'm still not willing to write you off. I know who you really are, even if you don't!"

Do caring long-sufferers in such circumstances some-times experience a temporary loss of patience? Yes! But such can be followed by the resumption of the outstretched arms toward the resistors. These resistors may be rebellious teenagers, an errant spouse, a sister full of self-pity, a pre-occupied careerist—all heedless of their exclusionary effects on others. Nevertheless, the loving long-sufferer will not go away, even when the objects of his concern entreat him to leave. It seems that some stubbornly insist on touching the bottom before even a slight upward momentum occurs. Painfully watching the long procrastinating and needless descent can be so anguishing. President Spencer W. Kimball put it so well:

"Procrastination—thou wretched thief of time and opportunity!

"When will men stand true to their one-time inspired yearnings?

"Let those take care who postpone the clearing of bad habits and of constructively doing what they ought. 'Some day I'll join the Church,' says one. 'I'll cease my drinking soon,' says another. 'One day I'll smoke no more,' others pledge. 'Some day we'll be ready for our temple sealings,' promise a delayed-action husband and wife. 'Some day, when they apologize, I'll forgive those who injured me,' small souls say. 'Some day I'll get my debts paid.' 'We'll get around soon to having our family prayers, and next week we'll start our home evenings.' 'We shall start paying tithing from our next pay check.' Tomorrow—yes, tomorrow."[10]

It is the true long-sufferer who waits with patience at the foot of the self-constructed crosses of those who insist on crucifying themselves and their possibilities. Nevertheless, the long-sufferer maintains the quiet heroism of hope, even though receiving so little appreciation from his beneficiaries.

Vicariously bearing our sins—whether bright or faded pink—Jesus, in fact, descended below all things in order that He might personally comprehend all things (D&C 88:6). Yes, we worship Jesus because *He is,* but we also worship Him because of what *He is like,* including His perfect attribute of long-suffering (Exodus 34:6–7). We ponder His sobering invitation, "What manner of men [and women] ought ye to be? Verily I say unto you, even as I am" (3 Nephi 27:27).

But will God's long-suffering finally fail anyway? Will it merely be seen by some mortals as His having given it "a good try?" Emphatically, no! Actually, God will succeed in working with humanity until all have had every chance. Perfect mercy and perfect justice will have prevailed—about which none will later complain! Instead, on Judgment Day all will affirm that God is perfect in His justice (Mosiah 16:1; 27:31; 29:12).

This collective but individual confessing will be unforced and will be expressed with great gratitude, including by those who will inherit the telestial kingdom which, though lesser, will still have a glory which "surpasses all understanding" (D&C 76:89). All will receive according to their wills and desires, including life in that kingdom (Alma 29:4). Divine long-suffering ensures such ultimate justice!

It is no wonder that we reverently worship our long-suffering Lord while also admiring and respecting the emulative, mortal long-sufferers. Though we would sometimes salute the latter—but without distracting them, because we see how they are so "anxiously engaged" (D&C 58:27)— their long-suffering nurtures those with short spans of spiritual attention. Those who so minister are patient even with those whose idealism has soured into cynicism and sarcasm.

Besides, within that cynicism are tracings of what once was and what could be again. Their very sarcasm sometimes shows how much their hopes have shrunken. Moreover, the errant who reject or abuse long-suffering are making their repentance ever more difficult. Each layer of scar tissue makes fresh soul surgery more difficult.

Therefore, while the rebellious try the capacity of those who strive to be long-suffering towards them—and limits do need to be set at times, with customized rebukes—yet, though unappreciated, the frequently disappointed long-sufferers remain strangers to self-pity. They are so giving, they would not think of giving up. Yes, occasionally gross events may understandably cause them to take a startled step backwards. But even when the rebellious act out further their selfish psychodramas, the friends do not turn away. They are "firm" in the Spirit (Alma 27:27; Helaman 15:8; Moroni 7:30; Jacob 4:18).

Even when such friends reprove with sharpness, the sharpness has the unmistakable tang of love. Long-sufferers know that ultimatums rarely are desideratums. While they do not care to appear as heroes and heroines on the evening news, they meekly bear the good news of the gospel of deserved forgiveness.

Long-sufferers are really something because they think the errant and unrepentant are really something—something worth saving. No wonder the long-sufferers will one day stand as meek saviors on Mount Zion, there to praise forever God's long-suffering and also to witness His perfect justice.

5

"O . . . THE JUSTICE OF OUR GOD!"

Ever to be juxtaposed with God's long-suffering is the reality that "his judgments are just," which is both sobering and emancipating (Mosiah 16:1; Alma 12:15; 2 Nephi 9:17). Among the many things for which we should be deeply grateful, though we cannot fully comprehend them, are God's perfected attributes of justice and mercy. Not only will every knee bow and every tongue confess that Jesus is the Christ (Mosiah 27:31) but on that judgment day a massive, confessional acknowledgment will indicate clearly that the justice of God is perfect and that He is merciful:

"We must come forth and stand before him in his glory, and in his power, and in his might, majesty, and dominion, and acknowledge to our everlasting shame that all his judgments are just; that he is just in all his works, and that he is merciful unto the children of men" (Alma 12:15).

"The time shall come when all shall see the salvation of the Lord; when every nation, kindred, tongue, and people shall see eye to eye and shall confess before God that his judgments are just" (Mosiah 16:1).

In ways we cannot now fully understand, such perfect justice is possible because an omniscient God truly knows what we know. Furthermore, He also knows the intents of our minds and hearts (D&C 6:16; Hebrews 4:12). He likewise knows our conceptual as well as our environmental limitations. He knows our genetic endowments. He knows the circumstantial interplay of opportunities and limitations. Reassuringly, He also knows our infirmities, sicknesses, pains, and sins (Alma 7:11–12).

Additionally, God has given to every individual the light of Christ. "That was the true Light, which lighteth every man that cometh into the world" (John 1:9). But God's original bestowal requires our maintenance to preserve its full power:

"And the Spirit giveth light to every man that cometh into the world; and the Spirit enlighteneth every man through the world, that hearkeneth to the voice of the Spirit" (D&C 84:46).

Whatever the measure of our individual discernment, it is judged against our deeds—good and bad—including our responses to the many calls of conscience. God thus can make all the necessary allowances, as He judges ever so justly our mortal performance. He gives us space or time in which not only to choose but also to repent and to change (2 Nephi 2:21; Alma 12:24; 42:5). In fact, in His plan, finally mercy "overpowereth justice" (Alma 34:15).

For reasons we may not have fully considered, would we not want God's justice to prevail anyway, even with any price we might personally have to pay? Were it not so, could we truly feel fully at home in His kingdom? Thus, even in the demands of His justice, one can sense His discerning love for His children.

It is in the context of His perfect justice and mercy that we may anticipate the moment before the judgment bar of God. By then, we will understand more fully *who* we are and *what* we might have done—especially *how* very much God loves us and has loved us for so very long. Indeed, we were with Him in the beginning, and He will act consistently with what we have known Him to be for a long, long time! (D&C 93:29).

Any shame or joy to be felt by us at that time of judgment, therefore, will occur when we recall our deeds with a "bright recollection" and a "perfect remembrance" (Alma 11:43; 5:18). Having been free to choose for ourselves, how can any complain?

All this foretells the ultimate reconciliation of the agency of man and the justice and mercy of God. Meanwhile, however, God pleads with us to choose the path of greatest happiness because He loves us. But He will not force us.

Any indifference toward Him by us we will finally see in the context of His constant caring for us. No overt or extensive scolding need necessarily come from Him on that occasion when we see "things as they really are" (Jacob 4:13). Any shame we feel will be felt because we will understand so much better then the benefactions of His steady love for us—a love which few will have fully reciprocated. Rather than scolding sternness, we will feel His unsurpassed kindness and tenderness—even as judgment is meted out. We will see how He has waited for us with open arms, the very arms and embrace which so many will have earlier rejected (Mormon 5:11; 6:17).

Meanwhile, before those grand and culminating events, there will be the second coming of the Savior, preceded by the appearance of old-fashioned fear in that midnight moment of time.

Worldly sorrow is never adequate, however, even if, at first, it resembles the real thing.

"When I, Mormon, saw their lamentation and their mourning and their sorrow before the Lord, my heart did begin to rejoice within me. . . .

"But behold this my joy was vain, for their sorrowing was not unto repentance, because of the goodness of God; but it was rather the sorrowing of the damned, because the Lord would not always suffer them to take happiness in sin.

"And they did not come unto Jesus with broken hearts and contrite spirits, but they did curse God, and wish to die. Nevertheless they would struggle with the sword for their lives" (Mormon 2:12–14).

So much of the ungodly sorrow we see is actually "the sorrowing of the damned." Each of us knows to a sufficient degree, even as we do wrong, that we are consciously doing wrong. God knows to a perfect degree, and His justice will be deservedly felt!

Though we cannot now be fully aware of it, how carefully gauged is the reality that God and His perfect judgment and justice take into account the interplay of so many factors in life and our performance therein. He knows perfectly the specific and individual constraints, "the tether and pang of the particular."[1] He knows our deeds and thoughts perfectly. Thus, how we perform in this second estate will be judged along with how we performed in the first estate, providing a sufficient basis with enough and to spare for perfect divine justice and judgment.

God is pervasively and lovingly in the details of things yet does not constrain our moral agency in any way. Rather, in His perfect love and awareness, He pays perfect and strict attention to details, and His influence is felt in many ways that are quite remarkable even in what seem to be the smallest of life's episodes. Why should we be surprised? Has He not told us that a hair shall not fall from the head unnoticed or a sparrow fall from the air? (Matthew 10:29–30). His divine attention is clearly far beyond our comprehension, but it is nevertheless a reality of which He has reassured us (Matthew 7:20–23).

In God's perfect justice, all things are considered. All moments—and moments are the molecules which make up eternity—are factored in. Each day, drop by daily drop, our lives provide a sufficient record and basis for divine judgment. Added thereto is the great safety net of opportunity in the spirit world, because its spreading will be the final rounding out of the chance for *all* to choose (D&C 138:30).

Meanwhile, do we all have the chance to serve as a prime minister of a nation? No, of course not! Do we all serve in situations of fame and high visibility? No! Do all enjoy wealth? No! Or excellent health? No! Nevertheless, do we all have sufficient chances to overcome with what has been allotted the portion of the world in which we are located? (Alma 29:4). Yes! Do we all have chances to be loving of family and neighbors? Yes! However small our local samples may seem to be, they will be sufficient in forming a basis for God's perfect justice.

We soon learn, for instance, that the gospel net "gathereth of every kind" (Matthew 13:7). So, likewise, we find Heavenly Father's children across the planet living in situations of every kind. There is no way for us to know, quantitatively, what portion of mankind is in one niche or circumstance compared to another. But the array of attitudes is worth reflecting upon, if only as we seek to share the harvest of the Restoration with both idealism and realism.

1. "They understood not the dealings of the Lord" who created them (Mosiah 10:14; see also 1 Nephi 2:12).

Bereft of a basic understanding of Heavenly Father's plan of salvation, many such mortals are bewildered, confused, and even resentful of life. With so many lacking a crucial understanding of "the dealings of the Lord" with his children, little wonder attitudinal differences are sometimes so deep.

2. Some simply "know not where to find [the truth]" (D&C 123:12).

A vast group of people on this planet simply do not know where to find the truth. Their plight constitutes one element of the urgency which underlies missionary work.

3. Some "desire to know the truth in part, but not all" (D&C 49:2). This seems a strange posture at first, but it reflects why some receive only a "lesser portion of the word" (Alma 12:10–11). Some may actually not desire the added accountability.

Surprisingly, some are willing to settle for less and are content with knowing part of the truth. Perhaps this is so because they sense the potential impact, implications, and requirements of accepting *all* of the truth.

4. Many "stumble exceedingly," including by "looking beyond the mark" (1 Nephi 13:34; Jacob 4:14; see also 1 Nephi 14:1).

Once Jesus is bypassed in hearts, minds, and behavior, as when some look beyond that mark, then it is so easy to stumble. The Light of the World was sent into a dark world, and the world comprehended it not (John 1:5; D&C 6:21; 88:49).

5. Some, though honorable, are "blinded by the craftiness of men" (D&C 76:75).

A few really have been taken in conceptually or behaviorally "by the craftiness of men." This condition may not involve deep, interior wickedness; rather, some people have simply been overwhelmed by constrained niche thinking.

6. Some hear the gospel and believe, but many "[believe] it not" (Acts 28:24). Others "[do] not believe, because they saw . . . not" (Ether 12:3–5).

Some simply reject the gospel per se. Others attach hindering conditions to believing, such as demanding to see certain things before they will believe; they represent a growing and wide swath in the intellectual community. Insisting on seeing before believing obviously shrinks the possibilities. Paul had it right:

"But the natural man receiveth not the things of the Spirit of God: for they are foolishness unto him: neither can he know them, because they are spiritually discerned" (1 Corinthians 2:14).

Meekness matters and is central to the spiritual method, just as intellectual humility is central to the scientific method.

7. Some are indifferent to spiritual things because "I am rich, and increased with goods, and have need of nothing" (Revelation 3:17).

A degree of contentment, economically, is a large deterrent to people's receiving the gospel, much more so than some of us realize. Such individuals simply do not want to consider anything that ruffles the smoothness of life.

8. Some are estranged from Christ, being variously diverted. "For how knoweth a man the master whom he has not served, and who is a stranger unto him, and is far from the thoughts and intents of his heart?" (Mosiah 5:13).

This verse applies to all who have become estranged from Christ—not serving Him, not thinking about Him, and having no place for Him in their hearts. They are busy and may not be in *transgression,* but they are certainly in *diversion.*

9. "They were a people friendly one with another; nevertheless they knew not God" (Mosiah 24:5).

Many people are friendly, decent, and honorable, but they have no understanding of the character and purposes of God. Of this condition the Prophet Joseph said, "If men do not comprehend the character of God, they do not comprehend themselves."[2]

10. Some, happily, are "in a preparation to hear the word" (Alma 32:6).

These are the glorious moments when people are already in a preparation, thanks to the mercy of God. Some do inquire humbly: "O God, Aaron hath told me that there is a God; and if there is a God, and if thou art God, wilt thou make thyself known unto me, and I will give away all my sins to know thee" (Alma 22:18). The act of true conversion involves so much, and nothing more significant than being willing, as in this case, to "give away all my sins to know thee." The grace of God is best received by those who respond to the light of Christ, not by those who pull down the shades!

Workers in the vineyard need to keep their labors in positive perspective, too. Nephi, son of Helaman, wearied over the people's wickedness and wished he had lived in earlier days (Helaman 5:4). Yet, he still was part of eight thousand baptisms! (Helaman 5:17–19). We, too, may be discouraged at times and even nostalgic for better days, yet fail to see the ways in which the work goes quietly forward, though perhaps in our cases not on the scale of weary Nephi.

The restored gospel's fulness is so bold and encompassing it can remove various stumbling blocks (1 Nephi 14:1). It does so with the very "plain and precious things" which can reshape man's view of himself, God, life, and the universe by telling us of "things as they really are" (1 Nephi 13:28; Jacob

4:13). Its richness has special appeal—"enough and to spare" (D&C 104:17)—to reach the poor in spirit—the meek!

Each must expect customized configurations of challenges which will constitute one's portion of "all these things," some of which will be especially vexing (D&C 122:7). The entire rollout will reflect the perfect justness of God with His perfect capacity to individualize life's curriculum.

The scriptures cited tell us about how all of God's children, at Judgment Day, will acknowledge the perfect justice of God. How could it be otherwise, given our agency and our eventually receiving according to our wills and desires? (Alma 29:4).

In that supernal setting, when every knee shall bow and every tongue confess that Jesus is the Christ, all will likewise acknowledge that God is God, including even those who have lived "without God in the world" (Mosiah 27:31). Having been free to choose for ourselves how we live here and now, we will in effect also have chosen where and how we will live in the there and then. This will be the breathtaking outcome constituting the ultimate reconciliation of the agency of man and the justice and mercy of God!

Meanwhile, however, God pleads with us to choose the path of greatest happiness, because He loves us. But He will not force us.

When we think of the preeminence of the Father and the Son and Their grandeur, which will be so demonstrably obvious on the day of judgment, we might ask how could some have failed to choose aright and to conform fully? Though it will be too late by then, is it also possible, when we are confronted in that vast panorama of confessional acknowledgment by "things as they really are, and of things as they really will be" (Jacob 4:13), that even then some will still desire to live other than with the Father and the Son?

The kingdoms granted by God will be kingdoms granted in consequence of all of each one's previous desires and choices. Many will have been unwilling to pay the costs of discipleship in the second estate. Thus, is it also possible that some will still not really desire to pay the post–Judgment Day costs of discipleship necessary for those who inherit the celestial kingdom?

As we think of the things to be variously allotted to Heavenly Father's children on the day of judgment (Alma 29:4), carefully we note the revelation about how the natural man simply cannot abide the presence of God (D&C 67:12). Certain people would "shrink from the presence of the Lord" (Mosiah 2:38); some would "hide . . . from the face of him that sitteth on the throne" (Revelation 6:16).

There is so much to consider as to what will happen in process of time. For example, one day the worthy members of the tribe of Judah, "after their pain" (D&C 133:35), will be admitted to the presence of the Lord forever and ever (D&C 76:118).

Obviously, a determining and defining moment lies ahead for all mortals. Yet that defining moment turns on our choices today.

Those who in the here and now have never sincerely sung with their souls "abide with me; 'tis eventide"³ are not likely to plead, subsequently, "abide with me" everlastingly. They will actually not want to be in His presence forever, because their confidence will not "wax strong in the presence of God" (D&C 121:45). The righteous, however, can have a "boldness in the day of judgment" (1 John 4:17).

Perhaps, therefore, that supernal scene will not be solely one of shame, guilt, and deep regret. The generous mansions once offered are not those wherein many would feel at home anyway. Likewise, celestial beauty and the divine music would be undesirable for so many, because of their own developed tastes and choices.

Yet, who would desire it to be otherwise more than would the Father, with all of His children having lived now so as to feel confident in His presence then and wishing to live with Him forever?

When all are finally settled in, according to the justice of God, our wills and desires will have prevailed, a fact we will not contest, given the consequences of our cumulative choices (Alma 29:4). Hence, Jesus will have been perfect in His advocacy, and the Father will have been perfect in His justice and mercy. Otherwise, the joy of the Father and the Son could not be truly full. Lesser outcomes, clearly chosen, cannot hold hostage Their celestial joy, especially when even the glory of the telestial kingdom will "surpass all understanding" (D&C 76:114). The plan of happiness will have delivered to each and all the measure of happiness they desired and could actually abide.

6

"THESE THINGS"

W hen imprisoned in Liberty Jail, the suffering Prophet Joseph Smith was counseled not merely to survive but to endure well. There he received important and consoling revelations about the tutoring nature of this mortal experience, including these well-known words: "All these things shall give thee experience, and shall be for thy good" (D&C 122:7; 121:8).[1] This wintry verse is instructive for us all, as we now focus briefly on two of its words: "these things."

First, many of life's afflictions and temptations are real but generalized, democratically built into the fabric and structure of mortality. These, wrote Paul, are "common to man" (1 Corinthians 10:13). One does not dismiss these challenges simply because they are widely shared, however.

Second, there are additional "things" which try us, too, and sometimes severely. These trials we actually bring on ourselves, though the suffering is just as real. For example, people can enclose themselves in self-constructed prisons of appetites and attitudes. In fact, we are imprisoned by whatever we are in bondage to, "for of whom a man is overcome, of the same is he brought in bondage" (2 Peter 2:19). There are so many such prisons!

A third category of "these things" consists of added tutorial trials and customized challenges. These might consist of health or economic problems, or the continuing insensitivity of a marriage partner, or a lack of appreciation from one's children, etc. Embedded in the "tether and pang" of these "particular" situations may be some of life's most defining moments.[2] If endured well, each of these experiences can contain the clinical material needed for tutoring, which can be especially for our good.

Such individualized opportunities may be deflected or rejected by us, of course. Or they may simply go unrecognized. Nevertheless, the moments were there, and they could have been seized "for [our] good" (D&C 122:7). Granted, such moments may be fleeting, but they can still be defining, depending upon our responses.

As in going from belief to faith and then on to knowledge, we can move onward incrementally in conquering "these things."

Though of themselves life's defining moments may seem minor, our wise responses can gradually increase our traction on the demanding path of discipleship. For instance, we can decide daily, or in an instant, in seemingly little things, whether we respond with a smile instead of a scowl, or whether we give warm praise instead of exhibiting icy indifference. Each response matters in its small moment. After all, moments are the molecules that make up eternity, affecting not only ourselves but others, because our conduct even in seemingly small things can be contagious.

"The current of life is made up of small springs, streams, and rivulets, or rather of little incidents which in the aggregate constitute the character of man here on earth. So small a thing as a kind word timely spoken to the sorrowful and afflicted often results in great good, and secures the esteem and gratitude of those to whom it may be addressed, while an ill word may do much harm."[3]

When we decide, for example, to be understanding instead of abrupt, the other party, in turn, may happily decide to hold on a little longer rather than give way to resentment. Whereas some contagious physical diseases are airborne, spiritual contagiousness can be attitude borne. Love, patience, and meekness can be just as infectious as rudeness.

So it is that we learn not only "precept upon precept" but also experience by experience (D&C 128:21). Experience actually remains the workhorse way of learning and also of further verifying the truth. Regardless, if we are meek, the Lord's "grace is sufficient" (Ether 12:26), thereby helping us in meeting these moments gracefully and productively. Good can come from them, difficult and stressful though they may be (D&C 122:7).

Later on, when we have better perspective, as President Brigham Young said, we will consider all of our mortal "losses, crosses, and disappointments, [and] the sorrows," in the context of eternity, and we will "exclaim, 'But what of all that? Those things were but for a moment.'"[4] Right now, however, we are in the midst of our intense though "small moment" (D&C 122:4; 3 Nephi 22:7).

When Jesus says His grace is sufficient for us, His unique and specific capacity for grace and empathy reflects all that He personally endured, including our sins, sicknesses, pains, and so forth (Alma 7:11–12; Ether 12:30). He who suffered the insufferable thus knows specifically and personally how to extend His grace and how to succor us (Alma 7:11–12). How different from a limited deity who might want to help his subjects but does not really know their pain or, even worse, how to succor them.

We, of course, are at risk in facing all types of trials in life's small moments as well as in the large ones. Hence, this apostolic counsel applies: "Wherefore let him that thinketh he standeth take heed lest he fall" (1 Corinthians 10:12). An automatic-pilot approach to daily life can thus be very risky.

We can, instead, be "added upon" drop by drop, until discipleship becomes "brim with joy" (Abraham 3:26; Alma 26:11). Yet doing so requires constant "faith unto repentance" (Alma 34:15). Patience can polish us even when we may feel at a particular moment that we are really being burnished.

Resilience is part of repentance, showing we have faith to try again—whether in a task or in a relationship. Resilience is really an affirmation of our true identities as spirit sons and daughters of God. We need not be permanently put down, because we can be "lifted up" by applying Christ's atonement (Alma 36:3). The "infinite atonement" thus can apply to our finite failures (Alma 34:12).

Our lives contain sufficient samples to provide enough variety of "these things." Genuine discipleship also means that we are always on stage. Yes, there are some private moments, but moving along the straight and narrow path is scarcely a solitary or an unobserved thing. Therefore, genuine meekness is required for enduring discipleship pursued on stage. Consider the candid anxiousness of the chariot-encircled young man saying in a defining moment to the prophet Elisha, "Alas, my master! how shall we do?" (2 Kings 6:15). Or, the believing and honest man who openly acknowledged to Jesus, "Lord, I believe; help thou mine unbelief" (Mark 9:24).

Therefore, "these things," though variously configured,

feature a precious process, one in which we are doing and becoming simultaneously. Moreover, sufficient unto each discipleship are the opportunities thereof!

When we sometimes seek validation of our worth as individuals, how wonderful it would be if we would but consider what we *are* more than what we *do*. Doing certain things, of course, clearly can enhance what we are, yet our mortal tasks and opportunities are not evenly distributed. Nevertheless, we each can become, amid varied circumstances and roles, more like Christ, especially in our capacity to love, to be meek, to be patient, and to be submissive.

Since we do not remember ordering them from life's menu, so many defining moments are actually compliments of the chef!

Spiritual memories can facilitate our progress in coping with our present portion of "these things." Said one expert on memory, "The function of memory in your life is not only quite remarkable, it is vitally necessary to your survival as a human being."[5]

Mark Van Doren has observed: "Memory performs the impossible for man; holds together past and present, gives continuity and dignity to human life. This is the companion, this is the tutor, the poet, the library, with which you travel."[6]

We can be stranded—personally and societally—by not letting the past play its rightful part, including by connecting the generations:

"The events for which one generation cares most are often those of which the next knows least: they are too old to be matters of personal recollection and they are too new to be subjects of study, they have passed out of memory and they have not got into the books."[7]

Hence, the in-between things can be lost unless wisely cultivated. It is not easy to describe what actually occurs when nostalgia stirs us productively and positively. We cannot fully account for what happens when our memories focus so intensely on a particular time or event which had seemingly slipped irrevocably away. Then, suddenly and briefly, we feel included and reminded again!

The mentoring of the Holy Ghost can bring to our remembrance spiritually significant things (John 14:26). Though the moments are brief, such infusions of feelings from the past revive us. There is a fresh and vivid sense of what was, stirring us as to what could yet be; the refreshing surf of recall has rolled over us, even if quickly. Furthermore, the scriptures can, as it were, enlarge our memories and incorporate such memories as if they were our own (Alma 37:8). Spiritual memories can thus give us a broader view of all "these things."

Perspective afforded by spiritual remembrance is a safeguard against a particularly vexing trend which adversely affects so many in this present and modern age. The seventh commandment, pertaining to chastity and fidelity, is so little valued. Memory lapses would be much fewer in this regard if some recalled their marriage covenants—made not all that long ago. Immorality, however, is not considered all that serious by many. If people are otherwise honorable or contribute anything worthy to society, they are given a free pass, so to speak, as to honoring chastity and fidelity. Some violators actually demand forgiveness before repentance.

Henry Fairlie wrote: "Lust is not interested in its partners, but only in the gratification of its own craving, not in the satisfaction of our whole natures, but only in the appeasement of an appetite that we are unable to subdue. . . . Lust dies at the next dawn, and when it returns in the evening, to search where it may, it is with its own past erased."[8]

To violate the seventh commandment, especially repeatedly, is actually a sign of stubborn self-indulgence. However commendable one's other contributions might be, to trivialize the seventh commandment shows conceptual anemia or an expectation of chronic self-excusal. Lot could tell us about trying to live in an immoral milieu, one "vexed with . . . filthy conversation," and there are filthy expectations, too (2 Peter 2:7).

Gertrude Himmelfarb has indicated: "Today's moralists have that . . . far-away, fanatical glint in their eye—'telescopic morality,' we might call it. Telescopic morality disdains the mundane values of everyday life as experienced by ordinary people—the 'bourgeois values' of family, fidelity, chastity, sobriety, personal responsibility. . . .

" . . . casual sexual intercourse is condoned, while a flirtatious remark may be grounds for legal action. It is a curious combination of prudery and promiscuity that is enshrined in the new moral code. An old Victorian would call it censorship without morality."[9]

Hence, attending the violation of the seventh commandment are shared cultural consequences, as Will Durant wrote:

"No one man, however brilliant or well informed can come in one lifetime to such fullness of understanding as to safely judge and dismiss the customs or institutions of his society, for these are the wisdom of generations after centuries of experiment in the laboratory of history. A youth boiling with hormones will wonder why he should not give full freedom to his sexual desires; and if he is unchecked by custom, morals, or laws, he may ruin his life before he matures sufficiently to understand that sex is a river of fire that must be banked and cooled by a hundred restraints if it is not to consume in chaos both the individual and the group."[10]

Some, if they believe at all in the coming reality and that "no unclean thing can enter into [His] kingdom," apparently expect eventual excusal, or, at worst, to be "beaten with [a] few stripes" (3 Nephi 27:19; Luke 12:48; see also 1 Nephi 15:34). Passing successfully through temptation-filled times and being righteous for the right reasons are those who really strive to follow Him, who had temptations of every kind and yet gave them "no heed" (D&C 20:22).

There is no way for us to be fully and spiritually submissive until our will is swallowed up in the will of the Father (Mosiah 15:7). Therefore, complying with the seventh commandment, which some regard as an inconvenience or an inconsequential requirement, becomes a major hurdle. Some almost insist on a right to engage in some unchastity and infidelity, justified because of their other contributions. They almost insist that both God and others overlook their unimportant peccadilloes. It is as if they demand a sensual surcharge for rendering service in any other respect.

Mark it down: If the seventh commandment really were that trivial, the adversary would not spend so much of his time encouraging its violation! Clearly, he recognizes his large and relatively easy harvest from its violation.

The fact is that although some demean the seventh commandment, its violation is actually a fundamental violation of the first and second great commandments—on which all the laws and commandments "hang," including the seventh (Matthew 22:40). Such transgression shows a fundamental disregard for God and for all the other individuals inevitably and adversely affected by unchastity and infidelity. Furthermore, if we are beckoned at all by the divine invitation to "become as little children . . . [in order to] enter into the kingdom of heaven," how can we excuse an indulgent, adults-only lifestyle? (Matthew 18:3; 18:4; Mosiah 3:19).

Historian John Lukacs perceptively warned years ago that sexual immorality was not merely a marginal development but, instead, was at the center of the moral crisis of our time.[11]

How can anyone lacking basic impulse control even presume to be submissive to God? Likewise, how greatly do such individuals esteem Christ's atonement, which graciously immortalizes them? Only by means of repentance can we eventually be "spotless" from sin (Alma 13:12). Or, perhaps a few spots do not matter? Adultery is okay, if one feeds the poor? Promiscuity is permissible, if one supports the arts?

Of course, it is through Jesus' merciful atonement that we may be forgiven at all, if we repent of our sins, including those of infidelity and unchastity. But for some to be cavalier about this commandment, as though keeping it were somehow beneath them, is a tragic mistake. Such a failure to bend to the Lord's will shows an unyielding posture of the soul. In fact, such an indulgent and stubborn lifestyle indicates a subtle state of rebellion, as if God can't really be serious when He asks us to practice self-denial and to checkrein our appetites! There is an arrogant contempt, however unconscious of itself, that pervades promiscuity. The tyranny of sexual immorality is truly oppressive, and it is not confined to perpetrators, thus requiring us to have added capacity to endure. Relativism can run riot:

"If there is nothing beyond death, then what is wrong with giving oneself wholly to pleasure in the short time one has left to live? The loss of faith in the 'other world' has saddled modern Western society with a fatal moral problem."[12]

So much depends on our capacity to confront our

particular configuration of "these things" but also on how we use the time allotted to us in this mortal estate. Of necessity, the process of discipleship is carried out in the process of time. One can scarcely consider the former without the latter.

CHAPTER

7

IN PROCESS OF TIME

W ithin mortality's carefully fixed parameters is another
of "these things" which are shared by all and which impinges
on us constantly. We call it time. Because we are eternal
beings, time is not our natural dimension. Hence, we cannot
help but notice its constant presence; it is part of the brief
and narrow mortal framework within which we are to overcome by faith, including faith in God's timing. Even so, we
are greatly helped by revelations that tell us much about
"things as they really are, and of things as they really will be"
(Jacob 4:13). Otherwise, time can so easily twist our take on
things. Little things can loom so large!

Courageous but meek, John the Baptist said, as the time
of his own special ministry neared its close, "[Jesus] must
increase, but I must decrease" (John 3:30). Unconcerned
with turf or the size of respective followings, John the Baptist
spoke a truth about a less-appreciated dimension of discipleship. If we are truly meek, we will not worry over dom-
inating a particular moment of time or turf. We will be more
concerned with what we *do* and what we *are!* Jesus com-
mended John, declaring a greater prophet had not been born

of women (Luke 7:28). Yet John "did no miracle[s]" (John 10:41).

True, some sincerely intend to nourish the gospel seed in their next season of life, but those procrastinated springs come late, if at all. Of course, we genuinely rejoice in late bloomers, as we do in returning prodigals. Mercifully, too, those who come in the last hour receive the same wages (Matthew 20:1–16). Yet, there will be no special door prizes at the final judgment for those most reticent and last on their knees or whose tongues are the last to confess!

Meanwhile, it is amazing to see how some believers are lured so easily out of their appointed place, like an athlete being taken out of position not by the superior skill or strength of an opponent but only by a mere head-fake!

So much of the world's distracting behavior shouts, in effect, *Notice me! Envy me!*—cries which are not really very far from *Worship me!* We hear it all the time from those who are superstars of this or of that. These self-centered emotions are a clear violation of the first and second commandments and are in sharp contrast to the ways of Him who said, "For I am meek and lowly" (Matthew 11:29).

In our time-conscious and ego-drenched world, such a lesson is worth savoring. Some treat time as if it somehow belonged outright to them and as if title to it were part of their turf. It is one thing to say "these are my days" (Helaman 7:9) in order to reflect determination to contribute righteously. It is quite another to feel that the Lord or others owe us a block of time and that we alone will call the cadence.

Unless we are meek and faithful, time, as experienced by mortals, can be viewed in such provincial ways. In the very same moment, for instance, some may be enjoying a long-awaited reunion, understandably desiring to prolong that precious moment and hold back the dawn. Still others, however, are longingly awaiting an impending reunion or with excruciating pain are awaiting death and, hence, would hasten the dawn. Understandably conscious of time and its seemingly slow passage are those tensely awaiting a crucial lab report and wishing the intervening hours to be over.

Life is so designed that we constantly feel time, for it encloses the cares and anxieties of the world. In fact, we must use much of our allotted mortal time to do the necessary and worthy work of the world. Furthermore, some of the cares of the world do require some caring about.

Nevertheless, such cares and chores can come to dominate life. We can easily find ourselves anxiously engaged in doing these lesser things, so that too little of ourselves and of our time are left over for the things of God. Our management of time tells us so much about the management of ourselves.

Inordinate attention to the cares and the work of the world causes the exclusion of the things of most worth, the latter being "omitted" and left "undone" (Matthew 23:23). Time's pressures can thus blur our focus, and we may find ourselves doing what time labels as urgent, even if it is not really important. We all try (usually in vain) to ignore the ringing telephone!

We really feel time and its prickly presence. Unlike birds at home in the air and fishes in the water, we in time are not in our natural dimension. No wonder the passage of time seems to go too slowly or too rapidly.

Life itself provides us a decisive experience with time and mortal momentariness, situated as the second estate is between a lengthy premortal and an everlasting postmortal existence. Compared to the first and third estates, the second estate is a mere afternoon. Yet, it is within temporal brevity that we now exercise our eternal agency to choose.

No wonder the mortal curriculum often seems so compressed! No wonder, too, given this short span, we should take up the tutoring cross daily, for we have "miles to go before [we] sleep."[1] Occasional restful reveries are permitted, but they do not last for long. We often yearn for more of a chance to savor things:

> I don't like a world of muchness,
> A world of push and fast and no;
> I like a world of swept-out bigness,
> Of let and think and slow.

One's mortal life, therefore, is brevity compared to eternity—like being dropped off by a parent for a day at school—but what a day!

Unsurprisingly, we ponder over how, with a later mere flick of the Divine wrist, "time is no longer" (D&C 84:100; 88:110).

Does "no longer" mean we will have passed through our own experience in the second estate, so that time will be over—but only for us? Will time still be needed for all those yet to pass through the second estate? We do not know the details, but the perspectives will be vastly different from those of the present in ways yet to be understood and experienced. In any case, working out our salvation in this elusive dimension—time—is unavoidable. Besides, we cannot fully understand time while we are inside it.

As consumers of time, we seldom find its passage to be just right. For instance, the seven long years Jacob worked for Rachel seemed to him to be "but a few days" (Genesis 29:20; see also D&C 121:7). On other occasions, we speak of how time can hang so heavy, whether we are amid a vexing challenge or mere boredom.

The scriptures, without elaboration, say that time is

measured only to man (Alma 40:8; D&C 84:100; 88:110). Indeed, we are constantly trying to measure time with clocks and calendars. Yet, as Sheldon Vanauken wrote so well, "We cannot love time. It spoils our loveliest moments."[2] Life's seasons come and go so quickly. We can even remember when summer used to be three months long!

Even so, would we droop in performing our duties without the prickly, prodding presence of time? Would unending reveries cause us to become lost in lassitude instead of rigorously pursuing our journeys back to our eternal home?

The revelations tell us that in the presence of God "all things . . . past, present, and future, are continually before [Him]" (D&C 130:7)—a condition which Joseph Smith called "one eternal 'now.'"[3] The revelations thus permit us to access certain sovereign truths. We need not be solely confined to the mere facts of the day with their short shelf lives.

Blessed are those who in the midst of all "these things" not only endure well but also use time well, by discerning between things portable and eternal on the one hand and the self-extinguishing things of the mere moment on the other. Surely part of choosing consists of learning to look at things longitudinally—through the lens of the gospel. The wise use of our time, guided by eternal truths, can spur this process and help to ensure that "all these things . . . shall be for [our] good" (D&C 122:7).

Malcolm Muggeridge wrote perceptively: "There is Time and there is Eternity. Because we are creatures of Time, what happens from moment to moment, from century to century, seems of crucial importance; because we are creatures of Eternity these happenings seem as unsubstantial as white clouds drifting across a summer sky. . . .

"Some balance or compromise has to be found between these two moods. If life is only unreal it is melancholy.

Wonder at its unreality soon gives place to bitterness of spirit. . . . On the other hand, if buses and newspaper headlines and the man winding up clockwork pigs, all that happens, represent the whole significance of life, it is equally intolerable. For what does happen? I look backwards and see for individuals and societies a round as monotonous as the seasons of rising and falling hopes; I look forwards and see the same process continuing."[4]

Sensitivity to seeming repetitiveness, unless we understand the plan of salvation and God's character and purposes, can be described as monotonous as the seasons. Yet, God Himself has said, "[My] course is one eternal round" (D&C 35:1). His eternal round is filled with redemptiveness, mercy, and love. How we regard it all is what matters, along with how we fill our own days and years and whether or not we are submissive to the purposes of Him who oversees this eternal round (1 Nephi 10:19). His purposes and plan include the glorious resurrection, when body and spirit are inseparably connected, bringing a fulness of joy.

No wonder the Restoration and its truths give us what Peter prophesied would be the "times of refreshing"! (Acts 3:19). Through those truths, we can see things afresh with a plain and precious perspective, for the "limits of time [we step] o'er."[5]

The trials which come amid time include the anguishing deaths of loved ones, underscoring aching emptiness. These, too, can enhance our spiritual perspectives amid "these things." The spiritual space loved ones have vacated can bring its own form of inventorying. Time helps us to count even more accurately what we once had. Mercifully, we can have it again! Meanwhile, however, could our later reunions really be fully appreciated without the preceding experiences of separation? Again, we see the relevance of God's plan—in process of time.

We see each other in process of time, which means we see each other in process of discipleship. This process includes the faltering, the stumbles, the triumphs, the enduring well, and so many other commendable things. Still, given the significance of discipleship, efforts to measure it are difficult, because so many important things are unmeasurable to us.

With regard to our physical health, there are some *vital signs,* such as pulse, blood pressure, respiration, and temperature. Measuring these may seem routine but can be a valuable diagnostic tool and provide crucial indicators. So far as our spiritual health is concerned, there are some vital signs which, over the years, have proved to be significant indicators. Do we engage in personal prayer, search the scriptures regularly, and pay tithing, all the while becoming more like Jesus? Yet some resent the simplicity!

As to the latter, the Holy Ghost testifies of the Father and the Son and glorifies Christ (John 16:14). Using whatever gifts and talents we have, we should do likewise!

Christ has told us a major way of glorifying and magnifying Him: "If ye love me, keep my commandments" (John 14:15). Implicitly, if we love Him but falter in keeping His commandments, we are to love Him enough to repent! Hence, repenting and improving are actually ways in which we truly glorify Christ!

Christ's atonement, being the central act of human history, benefits super sinners, sinners, and all of us as the makers of mistakes. Taking up the cross daily (Luke 9:23), rather than quarterly or semiannually, helps us in the isometrics of discipleship: the new man labors and struggles to put off the old, or natural, man, who will not go quietly, easily, or suddenly (Mosiah 3:19). Therefore, taking up the cross daily develops within us the extra strength we need to put him off with finality.

Actions that lie at the very center of Christ's atonement give us immense clues in terms of our own daily discipleship. Jesus was at His perfect best during the Atonement when things were at their very worst. Yet, when He entered Gethsemane, He "fell on his face" (Matthew 26:39). Further, we are told, He "poured out his soul unto death" (Isaiah 53:12; Mosiah 14:12). Moreover, He let his own will be "swallowed up in the will of the Father" (Mosiah 15:7). The imagery is staggering, made the more so by His own words after the Atonement, when He said He had felt "the fierceness of the wrath of Almighty God" (D&C 76:107).

The Atonement would not have been valid, however, if Jesus, standing in for us, had merely been sorry in our behalf. His atonement required infinite suffering in order to be an infinite atonement: vicarious and superficial sorrow would not have been enough! He revealed His awareness of the agony which lay ahead of Him when He said, "Would that I might not drink the bitter cup, and shrink" (D&C 19:18). For Him to have recoiled, pulled back, or failed to go through with the Atonement would, of course, have stranded all of us.

Pondering Christ's deep, deep devotion gives us crucial insights for our own discipleship. What are a few of the common mistakes we make in failing to apply the Atonement to our discipleship? Interestingly, God leaves us free to make these mistakes, and all of these mistakes reflect the need on our part for greater submissiveness to the Lord (Mosiah 3:19).

Perhaps our first mistake is to think that we own ourselves and also blocks of time. Of course, we have our agency and an inner sovereignty, but disciples are to sacrifice themselves to do Jesus' bidding with enough faith in God's timing to say, in effect, "Thy timing be done."

One disadvantage of thinking we own ourselves and blocks of time is that we then have a tendency to feel put upon by undesired and unexpected events and circumstances, as if we designed life's curriculum rather than responding to it.

A second mistake is failing life's little quizzes, thinking somehow we can cram and pass the final exam. The little quizzes are absolutely essential for us to pass, and when we fail, we need to draw upon the Atonement. The tests will come at us whether we pass them or fail them. Happily, the infinite Atonement can cover our finite mistakes, too.

It is not enough to perform reasonably well in the crunch times, during the spikes of suffering and stress, if we are then overcome in the long stretches.

We also make the mistake of not realizing that faith and patience are to be in tandem. "Nevertheless the Lord seeth fit to chasten his people; yea, he trieth their patience and their faith" (Mosiah 23:21). To be *tried* really means to be *developed,* which will happen if we are meek, the trials being part of the spiritual isometrics mentioned earlier.

We certainly need to focus on faith, of course, but likewise on patience, which is so vital to succeed while living in process of time. Impatience does not honor what is implied in the words *in process of time,* when we foolishly would have certain moments and seasons over and done with. By wishing to skip these, somehow we are ignoring their inherent possibilities for service and growth. We resemble airline passengers flying from coast to coast while quietly resenting the in-between spaces. But there are souls down there, not just sagebrush! So it is with life's seemingly in-between and routine spaces.

We make a mistake, too, if we feel put upon by events and circumstances, when some of these actually constitute the customized curricula for our development. Yet, we would push them away. Of course, we should petition for relief, and when it comes, we should give "more praise for relief."[6] But we should not be surprised if the relief sometimes fails to come.

Another mistake is failing to realize that so much of discipleship consists of the need for us to downsize our egos and diminish our selfishness. Genuine meekness is vital, a meekness which is not conscious of itself.

A further and common mistake is focusing on how we are free to choose, a fact in God's plan of salvation, while also assuming wrongly that we can choose to avoid the consequences of our choices. Jacques Bainville once said that we must want the consequences of what we want. There really are those among us who feel they can make certain choices and still not have to face the consequences of those choices.

Actually, no one honors our wills and desires more than God!

"A just God . . . granteth unto men according to their desire . . . ; yea, I know that he allotteth unto men, yea, decreeth unto them decrees which are unalterable, according to their wills, whether they be unto salvation or unto destruction" (Alma 29:4).

Many mortals also make the mistake of playing to the galleries. These may be peers, colleagues at work, being politically correct, or conforming to the praise and fashions of the world. Each of these galleries involves a mystic "they," played to so intensely and so regularly. But those galleries will be emptied on that judgment day when every knee shall bow and every tongue confess that Jesus is the Christ and all will acknowledge that God is God (D&C 88:104). Part of playing to such galleries includes the efforts by some who futilely insist on using some of their allotted time to try to conform the eternal truths of the gospel and the Church to the ways and thinking of the world.

It just won't work! Paul saw it clearly: "But the natural man receiveth not the things of the Spirit of God: for they are foolishness unto him: neither can he know them, because they are spiritually discerned" (1 Corinthians 2:14).

All of these mistakes are unworthy of Him and all that He did in Gethsemane and Calvary. These and other errors are rooted in our failures to understand what the Atonement cost and what it requires of us.

If by accessing the Atonement we glorify the perfect Christ, it will be done amid our imperfect but improving discipleships. No one would be more pleased to have it so than He!

The words of President Joseph F. Smith about the eternal virtues—though these are viewed as unexciting and unglamorous by the world—make such spiritual sense. The discipleship described brings abundant joy in a process that, when viewed from the outside, might seem routine:

"The opening of the heavens to you in marvelous manifestations will not establish you in the truth. We have abundant proof of that in the history of the Church. But the men and the women who are honest before God, who humbly plod along, doing their duty paying their tithing and exercising that pure religion and undefiled before God and the Father, which is to visit the fatherless and widows in their afflictions and to keep ones self unspotted from the world and who help look after the poor; and who honor the holy Priesthood, who do not run into excesses, who are prayerful in their families and who acknowledge the Lord in their hearts, they will build up a foundation that the gates of hell cannot prevail against; and if the floods come and the storms beat upon their house, it shall not fall, for it will be built upon the rock of eternal truth."[7]

Such are the high-yield, low-maintenance members of His Church, who use their time well. These dutiful disciples will not prevail, however, without having and using the gifts of the Holy Ghost, gifts which are not merely desirable but essential!

CHAPTER

8

THE GIFT OF THE HOLY GHOST

When President Martin Van Buren asked the Prophet Joseph Smith "wherein we differed in our religion from the other religions of the day, Brother Joseph said we differed in mode of baptism, and the gift of the Holy Ghost by the laying on of hands. We considered that all other considerations were contained in the gift of the Holy Ghost."[1] The Prophet's response is more significant than we may at first realize. Of all the brief summations which might have been given in responding to President Van Buren, this one was so appropriate, whether or not appreciated by the audience of one.

The gift of the Holy Ghost truly is one of the greatest blessings available to members of the Church. Actually, many *gifts* can come from the Holy Ghost. These are needed in every age and dispensation but certainly no less in the commotion-filled last days of the last dispensation. They are likewise needed at every stage and in every situation of life. After all, "The Holy Ghost . . . quickens all the intellectual faculties, increases, enlarges, expands, and purifies all the natural passions and affections, and adapts them, by the gift of wisdom, to their lawful use. It inspires, develops, cultivates and matures all the fine-toned sympathies, joys, tastes, kindred feelings, and affections of our nature."[2]

No wonder we are instructed to "seek ye earnestly the best gifts"! (D&C 46:8). Everyone is given a gift, but we are not limited to just one (D&C 46:11). Moreover, Paul urges us, regarding that which lies latent, to "stir up the gift of God, which is in thee" (2 Timothy 1:6).

Yet, for different reasons, many of us live far below, or are unaware of, our privileges! "Because of their faith in me at the time of their conversion, [they] were baptized with fire and with the Holy Ghost, and they knew it not" (3 Nephi 9:20).

If, as Nephi did, we liken to ourselves the scriptures pertaining to certain of those gifts, we can surely be further blessed (1 Nephi 19:23).

Let us begin with what is salvationally essential: baptisms by *water* and *fire* are both absolutely essential for our salvation.

"For John truly baptized with water; but ye shall be baptized with the Holy Ghost not many days hence" (Acts 1:5).

"And behold, whosoever believeth on my words, them will I visit with the manifestation of my Spirit; and they shall be born of me, even of water and of the Spirit" (D&C 5:16).

"Thou shalt declare repentance and faith on the Savior, and remission of sins by baptism, and by fire, yea, even the Holy Ghost" (D&C 19:31).

Likewise fundamental is the role of the Holy Ghost in the Godhead. He "witnesses of the Father and the Son," and He *glorifies* Christ (2 Nephi 31:18; John 16:14). Ever relevant, this glorification of our Savior is vital in the last days, when so many, as in meridian times, esteem Jesus as "naught" (1 Nephi 19:7).

This majestic meekness of the Holy Ghost in the midst of bestowing His mighty gifts also tells us something of His personality, for He gladly witnesses and glorifies. Therefore, at the center of the gifts of the Holy Ghost is His unique witnessing of Christ's atoning act, history's greatest emancipation:

"To some it is given by the Holy Ghost to know that Jesus Christ is the Son of God, and that he was crucified for the sins of the world" (D&C 46:13).

In today's world, too many admire Christ and His teachings but do not really know who He is and what He has really done. An illustration of the need for the witness of the Spirit about Jesus can exist close to home. Of Jesus and his family, we read, "For neither did his brethren believe him" (John 7:5).[3] "Brethren" refers to family members, as in "his mother and his brethren" (Matthew 12:46). Of Jesus' four brothers, either James was not included in this reference or he later changed, because Paul speaks of "James the Lord's brother" as being one of the apostles (Galatians 1:19).

Jesus was not the only prophet to be without honor among some members of his family—as well as in his own country (Matthew 13:57). One wonders in the absence of more divine data if the ordinariness and the day-to-day routineness kept certain loved ones from fully recognizing and believing Jesus? Clearly, some neighbors were not overly impressed: "Is not this the carpenter's son?" (Matthew 13:55). Perhaps even in less than messianic circumstances it takes special humility to recognize a prophetic or apostolic role within a family.

The specific roles of the Holy Ghost are matched by His specific capacities. For instance, only with divine deftness can He truly reach people in their varied cultural, attitudinal, and vocational niches, including those self-contented who are "rich, and increased with goods, [who] have need of nothing" (Revelation 3:17). He can, for example, reach the otherwise contented who are "friendly" one with another but who do not know about God (Mosiah 24:5). The Holy Ghost mentors still others who then become precious prospects "in a preparation to hear the word" (Alma 32:6).

The Holy Ghost will teach us, providing perspective about "things as they really are, and . . . things as they really will be" (Jacob 4:13; D&C 39:6; 75:10). This sense of proportion is needed daily! Not only does He reach mortals in their many niches, but the Holy Spirit "searcheth all things, yea, the deep things of God," and this must be so because the "things of the Spirit of God . . . are spiritually discerned" (1 Corinthians 2:10, 14). The Holy Spirit is thus ready, if we are, to take us well beyond being superficial so that we can learn the things of most worth.

The ways in which the Holy Ghost teaches are many. More than once President Marion G. Romney echoed the following: "I always know when I am speaking under the inspiration of the Holy Ghost because I always learn something from what I've said."[4]

In such situations, the substance conveyed is significant, but so is our realization of what is happening!

The Holy Ghost will help us by transmitting our feelings, teachings, and testimonies to others—even when, inadequate of ourselves, we cannot speak "the smallest part which [we] feel" (Alma 26:16). In so many of life's situations, do we not genuinely yearn to be able to connect, especially with those we love the most? Or with others who have played special roles in our lives?

Speaking at a conference, President Brigham Young

noticed in the audience Brother Eleazer Miller, one largely lost to Church history. Of him, President Young declared:

"If all the talent, tact, wisdom and refinement of the world had been sent to me with the Book of Mormon, and had declared, in the most exalted of earthly eloquence, the truth of it, undertaking to prove it by learning, and worldly wisdom, they would have been to me like the smoke which arises only to vanish away. But when I saw a man without eloquence, or talents for public speaking, who could only say, 'I know, by the power of the Holy Ghost, that the Book of Mormon is true, that Joseph Smith is a prophet of the Lord,' the Holy Ghost proceeding from that individual illuminated my understanding, and light, glory, and immortality were before me. I was encircled by them, filled with them, and I knew for myself that the testimony of the man was true. There sits the man who baptized me, (brother Eleazer Miller)."[5]

This episode illustrates vividly this role of the Spirit: "Wherefore, he that preacheth and he that receiveth, understand one another, and both are edified and rejoice together" (D&C 50:22).

Thus, a future president of the Church was taught and touched, and he felt the Spirit like fire in his bones. Soon, Brother Young was sharing the fire. One week after his baptism, he gave his first sermon: "[After I was baptized] I wanted to thunder and roar out the Gospel to the nations. It burned in my bones like fire pent up, so I [commenced] to preach. . . . Nothing would satisfy me but to cry abroad in the world, what the Lord was doing in the latter days."[6]

Such supernal and personal moments are made possible by cultivating the Holy Ghost!

Another gift of the Holy Ghost, often less appreciated and less explored, is how He can bless us by guiding our very prayers. Have not all of us on occasion puzzled beforehand over how to frame our petitions? Hence, this candor and assurance:

"Likewise the Spirit also helpeth our infirmities: for we know not what we should pray for as we ought: but the Spirit itself maketh intercession for us with groanings [sighings] which cannot be uttered" (Romans 8:26).

How often we need this very help with our prayers, for although we know we should pray, we are not always certain as to that for which we should pray!

Additionally and expansively, the Holy Ghost will show us "all things what [we] should do," including both major and minor things (2 Nephi 32:5). This gift is so practical, for "we are of God. . . . Hereby know we the spirit of truth, and the spirit of error" (1 John 4:6). How often in life do we need help to detect the "spirit of error," which might otherwise carry the day, as well as to receive verification and direction? "And by the power of the Holy Ghost ye may know the truth of all things" (Moroni 10:5).

The Holy Ghost can give us such guidance: "The spirit of truth . . . will guide you in all truth" (John 16:13).

He can thus help us both in the defining moments as well as in what might be called life's gray zones of choices. Our decisions, after all, are not such contests as the choice between whether we will rob a bank or hold family home evening. At times we must choose among good options, "A_1" and "A_2." But we need help in order to attend to the "weightier matters" and do the things of "most worth" (Matthew 23:23; D&C 15:6; 16:4, 6; 2 Nephi 9:51).

The Holy Ghost will not only guide us as to the highest and best use of our time and talents but also help us to pace ourselves during the arduous journey of discipleship. King Benjamin gave us the "wisdom and order" test, and the Lord gave the "strength and means" test to Joseph and Oliver (Mosiah 4:27; D&C 10:4). We do need to know just how to pace and balance our discipleship in "wisdom and order."

The Holy Ghost will bring all things to our remembrance, especially the words of Jesus or about him (2 Nephi 32:3, 5; John 14:26; 15:26). This enhanced recall includes remembering to be true to our past, to our covenants, and to God, who has been proven "in days that are past"[7] (John 14:26; 2 Peter 1:13; 3:1; 2 Thessalonians 2:5; Alma 5:6). These things past can give us the needed courage and heart for the present journey.

As we reflect on how the Holy Ghost preaches to us from the pulpit of memory, we consider Alma's case, wherein he remembered the words of his father about the Atonement: "My mind caught hold upon this thought" (Alma 36:18). Our minds, in order to grasp, thus require a residue of past counsel and shared thoughts upon which to catch hold!

Remembrance also includes stirring up the grateful memories of goodly parents:

"Behold, my sons, I desire that ye should remember to keep the commandments of God; and I would that ye should declare unto the people these words. Behold, I have given unto you the names of our first parents who came out of the land of Jerusalem; and this I have done that when you remember your names ye may remember them; and when ye remember them ye may remember their works; and when ye remember their works ye may know how that it is said, and also written, that they were good" (Helaman 5:6; 1 Nephi 1:1).

The bottom line, "that they were good," surpasses so many lesser compliments and conclusions about us from our posterity; these words about being remembered as "good" should spur us on. What we remember, as well as remembering itself, requires help.

The Holy Ghost is titled the Comforter, who "filleth with hope and perfect love" (Moroni 8:26). Consider how many mortals are living in deep despair, without knowing hope or real love.

Consider how many have sprouted and endured for a season and then stopped short. The Holy Ghost can be with us to the end. He will help us to endure, a precious gift yet to be appreciated by many of us (D&C 50:5).

How supernal this gift: "I will impart unto you of my Spirit, which shall enlighten your mind, which shall fill your soul with joy" (D&C 11:13). How many, having become encrusted in routineness, are joyless? Truly, the gifts of the Holy Ghost are rich and relevant!

The Holy Ghost "persuadeth men to do good" (Ether 4:11). Diversion, exhaustion, and preoccupation cause so much goodness to go unexpressed by us, unfortunately at a time when so many "hands . . . hang down" (D&C 81:5). Is not such persuasion, when extra efforts by us are needed, one of the effective ways the Holy Ghost glorifies Christ? "Inasmuch as ye have done it unto one of the least of these . . . , ye have done it unto [Him]" (Matthew 25:40).

"God anointed Jesus of Nazareth with the Holy Ghost and with power: who went about doing good, and healing all that were oppressed of the devil; for God was with him" (Acts 10:38). To accomplish so much of this good in the workaday world, the Holy Ghost's method is often to tell us in our minds and in our hearts (D&C 8:2). How careful we should be, therefore, that "[our] thoughts" are not far from Jesus (Alma 37:36).

President Boyd K. Packer has counseled us that often when we receive guidance from the Holy Ghost, we get directions without explanation. No wonder we are to strive to have the Holy Ghost as our "constant companion"! (D&C 121:46). When, because of our neglect, He leaves us, we are surely incomplete disciples because we then fail, for instance, to make decisions under the influence of the Spirit while at the same time growing by virtue of our own experience and with regard to our capacity to choose (D&C 122:7; 121:39; 105:10; Alma 5:14, 26; Romans 5:4; Genesis 30:27).

More than we do, we should realize how all worthy Church members can be guided in their various callings and roles. May we encourage others to seek that guidance. Once when President Brigham Young began to give counsel and instructions by letter concerning an urgent matter, he ceased, as it were, almost in mid-passage, and wrote instead:

"But after all, advice to you on the above points is probably useless, for you have the privilege of enjoying the same Spirit upon which we all depend for intelligence in the present movements as in all other cases."[8]

Because the divine maxim is "nevertheless, thou mayest choose for thyself" (Moses 3:17), we are to learn to choose responsibly, yet in doing this we need help. We also need help regularly. The plan of salvation is designed to facilitate our learning to choose wisely when we opt for righteousness and eternal life instead of misery and death (2 Nephi 2:27).

In the early days of the Church, there were several petitions to the Lord to which He responded in a tutoring manner. On one occasion, the brethren needed a watercraft. The Lord responded that whether they made one or bought one, "it mattereth not to me" (D&C 61:22). It did matter to the Lord that some "take their journey speedily" (D&C 52:7).

In like manner, a question arose as to whether they should go by land or water. The Lord said they should do "according to their judgments" (D&C 61:22). A similar divine response was given to the question of whether some of the brethren should go in a group or two by two; they were told this was something for them to determine. On another occasion, as to the direction in which they should proceed, the Lord said whether it was east or west or north or south, it didn't matter; they could not go amiss, because so many opportunities awaited (D&C 80:3).

These incidents do not suggest any divine indifference whatsoever as to details. Rather, they illustrate how the mentoring of the Lord will surely guide us, but He expects us to use our own minds reliably and to develop them even further in our capacity to choose. Experience, therefore, can be a workhorse way of learning, as we develop our capacity to choose wisely under the influence of the Spirit.

"There are many things of much importance, on which you ask counsel, but which I think you will be perfectly able to decide upon, as you are more conversant with the peculiar circumstances than I am; and I feel great confidence in your united wisdom; therefore you will excuse me for not entering into detail. If I should see anything that is wrong, I would take the privilege of making known my mind to you, and pointing out the evil."[9]

Do we, therefore, need to worry about bothering the Lord? On the contrary, we are to pray over our flocks, crops, and fields (Alma 34:20, 24–25). We are to strive to have the Holy Ghost as our "constant companion" (D&C 121:46). Even so, given the timetable of the Lord, may we ask questions to which He will not yet respond? Yes! To a query concerning the time of the Second Coming, the Lord thus gave a partial answer and then said, "Let this suffice" (D&C 130:15). Martin Harris encountered a similar situation, from which we perceive a similar insight (D&C 5:29).

In addition to these scriptural examples, President

Brigham Young spoke about the need to develop our "inde-pendency"—not meaning, of course, to place any less reliance upon the Lord but to foster more simultaneous development of our divinely given gifts:

"Sometimes I think it quite strange that the children of men are so constituted as to need to be taught one lesson all the time, and again it is not so marvellous to me, when I reflect upon and understand their organization, and the designed effect thereupon of this state of probation. Men are organized to be independent in their sphere, are organized for an independent being, yet they have, as soldiers term it, to run the gauntlet all the time. They are organized to be just as independent as any being in eternity, but that independ-ency, in order for them to occupy a position in the sphere of an independent being having control over all things, must be proved and tried while in this state of existence, must be operated upon by the good and the evil."[10]

The counsel of President Harold B. Lee is likewise rele-vant: we need to gain personal experience by walking to "the edge of the light."[11]

No wonder the scriptures include such words as "we have learned by sad experience" (D&C 121:39). Jacob's father-in-law said he had learned by good "experience" that he was wise if he hearkened to Jacob (Genesis 30:27). Hence, our experience can mentor us, especially if we are meek and under the direction of the Spirit. We can be per-suaded, as were the Nephite stripling warriors by their expe-rience of having strong and spiritual mothers on whose spiritual knowledge they had come to rely. A crisis produced the same reflex. These young warriors "[did] not doubt [their] mothers knew it," showing yet another way of draw-ing upon experience (Alma 56:48).

Righteous parents and families who are influenced by the

Spirit can facilitate such mentoring. The general role families are to play is of considerable consequence. One observer wrote:

"We learn to cope with the people of this world because we learn to cope with the members of our family. Those who flee the family flee the world; bereft of the former's affection, tutelage, and challenges, they are unprepared for the latter's tests, judgments, and demands."[12]

When we think of nurturing families, understandably we usually think primarily of parents in whose homes the Spirit dwells. But children form a proactive part of the nurturing circle and are not merely the objects of the nurturing. One of their often unappreciated capacities is expressed in Alma:

"And now, he imparteth his word by angels unto men, yea, not only men but women also. Now this is not all; little children do have words given unto them many times, which confound the wise and the learned" (Alma 32:23).

An episode involving the resurrected Jesus with Nephite parents and their children illustrates this truth:

"And it came to pass that he did teach and minister unto the children of the multitude of whom hath been spoken, and he did loose their tongues, and they did speak unto their fathers great and marvelous things, even greater than he had revealed unto the people; and he loosed their tongues that they could utter" (3 Nephi 26:14).

Why should such an event surprise us, since we adults are to "become as little children" before we can "enter into the kingdom of heaven"? (Matthew 18:3).

If we are meek, then in order to guide us the Spirit can cut into what may seem on the surface a routine circumstance, one which we could normally handle ourselves. The Spirit could advise us that, perhaps unexpectedly, we need to be especially careful or to do this or to do that. When such a prompting happens, we should not be offended as to any implied lack in our own capacity but instead be grateful for the Holy Ghost's capacity.

Following his martyrdom, the Prophet Joseph appeared to President Brigham Young and said of the Spirit:

"Tell the people to be humble and faithful, and be sure to keep the spirit of the Lord and it will lead them right. Be careful and not turn away the small still voice; it will teach you what to do and where to go; it will yield the fruits of the kingdom. Tell the brethren to keep their hearts open to conviction, so that when the Holy Ghost comes to them, their hearts will be ready to receive it. They can tell the Spirit of the Lord from all other spirits; it will whisper peace and joy to their souls; it will take malice, hatred, strife and all evil from their hearts; and their whole desire will be to do good, bring forth righteousness and build up the kingdom of God. Tell the brethren if they will follow the spirit of the Lord they will go right. Be sure to tell the people to keep the Spirit of the Lord; and if they will, they will find themselves just as they were organized by our Father in Heaven before they came into the world."[13]

How crucial, therefore, it is for us to cultivate the Spirit in our lives, including in preparation for our lives in the spirit world.

CHAPTER

9

THE SPIRIT WORLD

Often Church members suffer from a lack of perspective, perhaps understandably, as to the vastness and intensity of the Lord's work in the spirit world. The scope is enormous! Demographers estimate that some sixty to seventy billion people have lived on this planet thus far. Without diminishing in any way the importance of the absolutely vital and tandem work on this side of the veil, we do need a better grasp of "things as they really will be" (Jacob 4:13). Otherwise, we can so easily come to regard family history as a quaint hobby and its resulting temple work as something we will get around to later.

Not only does the word *vastness* characterize the work there but so does *intensity*. Of course, we still lack many details and would like to know more. Even so, we ought to pay closer attention to what has been given about the spirit world so that we can truly "cite [our] minds forward" in appropriate ways (Alma 13:1).

Let us begin with paradise and Alma's description of that special destination to be reached after death but on the way to immortality and eternal life:

"And then shall it come to pass, that the spirits of those who are righteous are received into a state of happiness, which is called paradise, a state of rest, a state of peace, where they shall rest from all their troubles and from all care, and sorrow" (Alma 40:12).

Some derive from these words that *rest* means no work and merely languid passivity. In fact, the *rest* described is from the troubles, cares, and sorrows of this world.

To begin with, a certain peacefulness and restfulness will occur in paradise, because the faithful will see things with a more complete, restful, and reassuring perspective. Nonetheless, the faithful will soon be caught up fully and be "anxiously engaged" in the vast work underway in all the spirit world (D&C 58:27). So many of the cares and demands of the world which press upon us here and now, including doing the chores of this world, will not dominate us there. Hence, paradise will be, comparatively, "a state of peace." Furthermore, the spirit body will not suffer certain of the ills and constraints which now beset the mortal body. The result will be added zestfulness there, as described by Elder John Taylor:

"[Death] this dark shadow and valley is so trifling . . . [one is] passed from a state of sorrow [and] grief, . . . into a state of existence where I can enjoy life to the fullest extent as far as that can be done without a body. . . . I thirst no more, I want to sleep no more, I hunger no more, I tire no more, I run, I walk, I labor, . . . nothing like pain or weariness, I am full of life, full of vigor."[1]

Further illustrative of the consuming scope and intensity of the work there is the following exchange between the martyred Prophet Joseph Smith and President Wilford Woodruff:

"Joseph Smith continued visiting myself. . . . He said he

could not stop to talk with me because he was in a hurry. . . . I saw the Prophet again. . . .

"'Now,' said I, 'I want to know why you are in a hurry. I have been in a hurry all my life; but I expected my hurry would be over when I got into the kingdom of heaven, if I ever did.'

"Joseph said: ' . . . Every dispensation . . . has had a certain amount of work to do . . . Each dispensation has had ample time. . . . We have not. We are the last dispensation, and so much work has to be done, and we need to be in a hurry in order to accomplish it.'"[2]

The work being done there with such intensity, however, is not a random, hectic, and disorganized thing. Instead, unsurprisingly, it proceeds in a very orderly manner. Following is an account by President Heber C. Kimball, reflecting earlier conversations among members of the First Presidency—Brigham Young, Heber C. Kimball, and Jedediah M. Grant—given at President Grant's funeral in December 1856:

"[Brother Grant] said to me, brother Heber, I have been into the spirit world two nights in succession, and, of all the dreads that ever came across me, the worst was to have to again return to my body, though I had to do it. But O, says he, the order and government that were there! When in the spirit world, I saw the order of righteous men and women; beheld them organized in their several grades, and there appeared to be no obstruction to my vision; I could see every man and woman in their grade and order. I looked to see whether there was any disorder there, but there was none; neither could I see any death nor any darkness, disorder or confusion. He said that the people he there saw were organized in family capacities; and when he looked at them he saw grade after grade, and all were organized and in perfect harmony. . . . 'Why, it is just as brother Brigham says it is; it is just as he has told us many a time. . . .'

"He saw the righteous gathered together in the spirit world, and there were no wicked spirits among them. . . .

"'To my astonishment,' he said, 'when I looked at families there was a deficiency in some, there was a lack, for I saw families that would not be permitted to come and dwell together, because they had not honored their calling here.'"³ Families do not guarantee automatic individual salvation.

The vastness of the work in the spirit world of preaching the gospel is confirmed in the 1918 vision of President Joseph F. Smith, which was accepted by the Church in 1976 as a revelation. That work is proceeding, "even to all the spirits of men" (D&C 138:30). Billions and billions of them!

Likewise, although Jesus did not personally go among the wicked, He organized His work so it could go forward there, "even to all." Consider, however, Jesus' glorious welcome in paradise:

"While this vast multitude waited and conversed, rejoicing in the hour of their deliverance from the chains of death, the Son of God appeared, declaring liberty to the captives who had been faithful; . . .

"And the saints rejoiced in their redemption, and bowed the knee and acknowledged the Son of God as their Redeemer and Deliverer from death and the chains of hell.

"Their countenances shone, and the radiance from the presence of the Lord rested upon them, and they sang praises unto his holy name" (D&C 138:18, 23–24).

Therefore, an interesting constituency awaits us, such as those "who had died in their sins, without a knowledge of the truth" (D&C 138:32). This group is obviously very large!

None is to be left out, however, even those in the spirit

prison who once "rejected the prophets" or who are there "because of their rebellion and transgression, that they through the ministration of his servants might also hear his words" (D&C 138:32, 37).

What are all individuals to hear and to be taught?

"These were taught faith in God, repentance from sin, vicarious baptism for the remission of sins, the gift of the Holy Ghost by the laying on of hands,

"And all other principles of the gospel that were necessary for them to know in order to qualify themselves that they might be judged according to men in the flesh, but live according to God in the spirit" (D&C 138:33–34).

Understandably emphasized is vicarious baptism for the dead, because that ordinance is absolutely essential for their cleansing and salvation. Furthermore, the recipients can thereby qualify to become members of The Church of Jesus Christ of Latter-day Saints by developing sufficient faith and also by showing sufficient repentance in the spirit world.

Typically, in that connection, we here do not emphasize as much the other essential part of what can happen vicariously—confirming Church membership and the bestowal of the great gift of the Holy Ghost. Because the accompanying and essential ordinances remain to be accomplished vicariously on our side of the veil, it would be well if more of the intensity characteristic of work in the spirit world were displayed by us in mortality. Indeed, the gifts of the Holy Ghost also help recipients there to lend a hand and to function more effectively in the spirit world *after* they are empowered by the vicariously given gift of the Holy Ghost!

President Brigham Young described further the spirit world:

"They do not pass out of the organization of this earth

on which we live. . . . But where is the spirit world? It is incorporated within this celestial system."[4]

President Young also stated: "Is the spirit world here? It is not beyond the sun, but is on this earth that was organized for the people that have lived and that do and will live upon it. No other people can have it, and we can have no other kingdom until we are prepared to inhabit this eternally."[5]

The Prophet Joseph said: "When men are prepared, they are better off to go hence. . . . The spirits of the just are exalted to a greater and more glorious work; hence they are blessed in their departure to the world of spirits. Enveloped in flaming fire, they are not far from us, and know and understand our thoughts, feelings, and motions, and are often pained therewith."[6]

Brigham Young further observed as to the associational groupings there: "Yes, brethren, they are there together, and if they associate together, and collect together in clans and in societies as they do here, it is their privilege. No doubt they yet, more or less, see, hear, converse, and have to do with each other, both good and bad."[7]

Clearly, there are many other questions to which we do not have detailed answers. But, as has been set forth, we know considerable about the essential things: (1) the vastness of the work there, (2) its intensity, (3) its inclusiveness by sharing the gospel with all, (4) the orderliness with which the Lord carries out His work of mercy and justice in the spirit world, (5) the special status of those who are in paradise, (6) how those who may be emancipated from the spirit prison can then help to accomplish this work, and (7) the grouping together of people in what may have been some natural associations here that will persist there.

Sometimes in the Church we speak imprecisely at funerals and otherwise as if individuals who die go immediately to the celestial kingdom and are at once in the full presence of God. We tend to overlook the reality that the spirit world and paradise are part, really, of the second estate. The work of the Lord, so far as the second estate is concerned, is completed before the Judgment and the Resurrection.

Since those who go to the celestial kingdom include, as revealed, those who "overcome by faith" (D&C 76:53), the same efforts and triumph would need to occur in the spirit world before they receive resurrection and the entitlement to enter the celestial kingdom.

The veil of forgetfulness of the first estate apparently will not be suddenly, automatically, and totally removed at the time of our temporal death. This veil, a condition of our entire second estate, is associated with and is part of our time of mortal trial, testing, proving, and overcoming by faith—and thus will continue in some key respects into the spirit world.

Yet, do people who have been wicked and agnostic, when they pass through the veil of death, suddenly and fully realize that there is, in spite of their earlier skepticism, life beyond the grave? Do they thus have an advantage over those who have had to develop faith in mortality concerning that prospect? If, for instance, the same attitudes with which we die persist, then there will be no automatic or immediate flip-flop into a totally different way of thinking. Such can occur there, just as it does here, upon our accepting the gospel and responding with both faith and repentance (Alma 34:34). Again, our existence in the spirit world is part of the mortal sector of our Father's plan which culminates with the Judgment and the Resurrection.

Surely those just and honorable mortals who have done so well here with the light they have received are the most likely to respond in paradise and the spirit world, when the fulness of the light of the gospel is given to them there. Consider the comments of the Prophet Joseph Smith about the important role of spiritual knowledge:

"Knowledge does away darkness, suspense and doubt, for where Knowledge is there is no doubt nor suspense nor darkness. There is no pain so awful as the pain of suspense. This is the condemnation of the wicked; their doubt and anxiety and suspense causes weeping, wailing and gnashing of teeth."[8]

The "pain of suspense" apparently will necessarily operate to some extent in the spirit prison because of uncertainty—along with a price to be paid as part of repentance for transgressions. The Prophet Joseph also said:

"A man is his own tormentor and his own condemner. Hence the saying, They shall go into the lake that burns with fire and brimstone. The torment of disappointment in the mind of man is as exquisite as a lake burning with fire and brimstone. I say, so is the torment of man."[9]

The word *prison* carries with it the connotation of "a state of confinement," including a conceptual confinement. The Prophet Joseph Smith said, for instance, that God has "made ample provision for their redemption, according to their several circumstances, . . . whether in this world, or in the world to come."[10] Surely that declaration is emancipatory!

The Prophet also consoled: "God has administrators in the eternal world to release those spirits from Prison. The ordinances being administered by proxy upon them, the law is fulfilled."[11]

Likewise, the Prophet, when speaking of us and our chance to become "saviors . . . on Mount Zion," instructed as to how the merciful salvation for the dead "places the human family upon an equal footing, and harmonizes with every principle of righteousness, justice and truth."[12]

The Prophet Joseph declared that those who die in the faith in turn preach to those who have died "that they may live according to God in the Spirit and men do minister for them in the flesh and angels bear the glad tidings to the spirits and they are made happy by these means."[13]

Thus, we see from what is presently known concerning the work in the spirit world that its scope is enormous and its intensity real. Its justice and mercy reflect Heavenly Father's plan of salvation. But missionary work is work both here and there, though the latter proceeds on a much larger scale. We will surely have ample opportunities for service beyond the veil, when that time comes to each of us!

How marvelous it is that Heavenly Father gives to all full and generous recognition for all their good deeds and all their good qualities. Thus, we can all be judged justly out of the "book of life" (Revelation 20:12). Yet, God still requires of all obedience to His doctrines, ordinances, and covenants. Nicodemus, one of the best, was nevertheless told that no man shall enter the kingdom of heaven except he shall be born again (John 3:5). Jesus' baptism, and He was the Best, showed us His obedience and submissiveness to the Father with regard to that essential ordinance (2 Nephi 31:5–7). He, who might have been an exception, nevertheless pointed the way! The ordinances of salvation apply to all.

Thus, if not on this side of the veil, then in the spirit world to come, the gospel will be preached to all, including all transgressors, rebels, and rejectors of prophets, along with all those billions who died without a knowledge of the gospel (D&C 138).

The mercy of God will finally overpower justice for all. God gave agency to all. He extends His long-suffering to all, as He did in the days of Noah. He further reminds us, in the parable of the wheat and the tares, of the need for restraint and patience regarding the Second Coming (Matthew 13:29; D&C 38:12). To that very end, the Father determines the timing as to when the angels of heaven come down in judgment on the world.

He gave us our spirit birth, bringing the first estate to all. He gave the gift to us of mortality, or the second estate, where all might be "added upon," leaving one-third of the host free to be rebels! (Abraham 3:26; Revelation 12:4). He provides in the spirit world a continuum of mortality's probation, the great opportunity for all.

The specific desires of our individuals hearts will finally and ultimately be granted to all. How can we complain? Because He is a loving Father, at Judgment Day, all those who have lived without God in the world will acknowledge that God is God and all will acknowledge that God is just!

"Oh how great [is] the plan of our God!" (2 Nephi 9:13).

But how little, really, we would know of that divine plan without the Prophet of the Restoration, Joseph Smith!

10

THE PROPHET
JOSEPH SMITH

Having written and spoken extensively over the years, testifying to the remarkable ministry of the Prophet Joseph Smith, I give this further testimony with a different emphasis, mixed with a few past reflections. These fresh words come in my sunset days as additional reflections have brought me an even deeper appreciation for Joseph. By their very nature, these are simple and summational observations without extensive elaboration.

First, often read but perhaps not considered sufficiently as to their implications for his ministry, are these words in Joseph Smith's report of the First Vision: "And many other things did [the Lord] say unto me, which I cannot write at this time" (Joseph Smith–History 1:20). Which, if any, of those "many other things" were shared later with the Church? We do not know with precision, for we have no specific, itemized inventory. It should be remembered, therefore, that whether it was in the sunrise, mid-day, or sunset of his ministry, the Prophet Joseph received more revelations than he shared fully. In Nauvoo, Joseph said confirmingly, "It is my meditation all the day, and more than my meat and drink, to know how I shall make the Saints of God comprehend the visions that roll like an overflowing surge before my mind."[1] His concern for the Saints' comprehension was genuine even as the revelations were ongoing!

One can scarcely imagine facing such a unique challenge on top of everything else, especially given the huge harvest of the pangs and promises of discipleship during his ministry!

The Everest of ecclesiastical truth built from the translations and revelations of the Prophet Joseph Smith speaks for itself—it towers above the mere foothills of mortal philosophy. At times, Joseph's phonetic spelling, characteristic of the time, may have left something to be desired, but he certainly provided us with the essential grammar of the gospel!

Joseph was open, generous, and anxious to share. Yet, he knew there were still some things he could not share. Or, if shared, they might be distorted, contributing perhaps in some situations to Joseph's being "marred" as prophesied (3 Nephi 21:10). Moreover, Joseph Smith Sr., in a father's blessing given in December 1834, told his prophet son that he would be marred "for a little season" but he would eventually triumph as "thousands and tens of thousands shall come to a knowledge of the truth through thy ministry, and Thou shalt rejoice with them in the Celestial Kingdom."[2]

To *mar* suggests trying to make the object less attractive, at least on the surface. Church members should not be surprised, therefore, if enemies seek to mar prophets and the Church itself, by attempting to render them less attractive and influential, thus causing some to discount the Lord's work and His servants. One of the early Twelve, Elder Orson

Hyde, observed that the "shafts" intended for the Church "are always aimed at the head first."[3]

Being marred can be part of the experience of discipleship for many: "Blessed are ye, when men shall revile you, and persecute you, and shall say all manner of evil against you falsely, for my sake" (Matthew 5:11). If we as members are likewise marred while doing the Lord's work, it will prove to be yet another dimension of sharing the fellowship of Christ's sufferings (Philippians 3:10).

Good but imperfect prophets are especially likely to be slandered. Nor are they immune from trials. In fact, of the responsibilities of priesthood leaders, the Prophet Joseph Smith said, "The higher the authority, the greater the difficulty of the station."[4] President John Taylor further said, "God tries people according to the position they occupy."[5]

Near the end, the Prophet noted, "I never told you I was perfect; but there is no error in the revelations which I have taught."[6] The Prophet Joseph, then and since, has been subjected to intense mortal scrutiny. Yet, as prophesied, many in the world ever continue to "inquire after [his] name" (D&C 122:1).

The Lord on occasion chastised the good but nevertheless imperfect prophet for falling short (D&C 5:21). The Lord was tutoring—not indulgent—of Joseph, and Joseph recorded his own chastisement. He loved Joseph and called him, but God was also willing to correct him.

In the midst of his own allotted "these things," Joseph came only gradually—rather than instantly and fully—to appreciate all the intertwinings and all the implications of some of the deep doctrines which had come, almost surflike, through him, whether by translation or revelation (D&C 122:7). Why should anyone be surprised at the "precept by precept" process? (D&C 98:12).

How many times, for example, did Jesus tell the original apostles of the impending resurrection? (Mark 9:31–32; Luke 9:44–45; 18:33–34). Yet, only later, after experiences and events, did the doctrine dawn fully on the original Twelve:

"These things understood not his disciples at the first: but when Jesus was glorified, then remembered they that these things were written of him, and that they had done these things unto him" (John 12:16).

If, likewise, Jesus' parents did not fully comprehend at first what Jesus meant about his need to be about His Father's business (Luke 2:49–50), or the Twelve all of His declarations of His messiahship (John 8:25–27), or audiences His mention of "other sheep," the scattered fold (John 10:6)—why should not Joseph be granted adequate time for the further unfolding of his own full understanding?

A second sunset reflection concerns a matter which merited more consideration by me and sooner. Joseph, though a "choice seer," was on stage, so to speak, all the time (2 Nephi 3:6–7, 11, 14; D&C 21:1). Any imperfections, real or seeming and however minor, were visible. Furthermore, the compressed time of his ministry, containing so many crises, often gave him little opportunity for adequate explanations of this or that. President Lorenzo Snow, meekly but instructively, said of the Prophet's imperfections:

"When I saw the weaknesses and imperfections in him I thanked God that He would put upon a man who had these imperfections the power and authority which he placed upon him . . . for I knew I myself had weakness and I thought there was a chance for me."[7]

Worldly critics, of course, apply secular screens. The natural man has his own frame of reference. Being nonspiritual, the natural man automatically attributes his own motives to others. Therefore, no allowance is made for things beyond the grasp of the natural man—something, ironically, so natural!

Take, for instance, the classic and ancient intellectual position of many about how mortals cannot know the future and that which is to come. How, then, do such skeptics explain the remarkable 1832 prophecy by Joseph Smith concerning the impending civil war given years before it began? (D&C 87). Their response would likely be the same as that given by others in another time, that prophets had "guessed" correctly (Helaman 16:16).

Therefore, in judging someone like the Prophet Joseph Smith, the natural man will use his ready-made sociological and sensual explanations for everything. Or, even when some praise is meted out, it tends to acknowledge that Joseph was "charismatic" or that Brigham Young was "a great colonizer," and so on, which is in a way like being praised with faint damns. Thus, in judging the Restoration, for instance, no secular allowance is made for anything such as a "marvelous work and wonder" (2 Nephi 27:26).

Granted, those with spiritual frames of reference proceed in their own ways, too. Therefore, such different beginnings as between the natural man and the man of Christ result in sharply different conclusions. We should not be surprised that this is the case. Hence, it is nonsense for believers to try to squeeze and spin spiritual things to fit into or to appeal to the natural man, as if hoping somehow to appease, to please, or to accommodate the world. Paul saw the futility of doing this, noting that the "things of the Spirit of God . . . are foolishness" to the natural man (1 Corinthians 2:14).

Joseph Smith marched to a different and Divine Drummer!

Thus, those who try to drive wedges between the

Prophet Joseph and his Lord, who called him, will only end up finally creating distance between themselves and the Lord! Those who revile Joseph Smith will not change Joseph's status with the Lord—merely their own! (2 Nephi 3:8).

A third reflection expresses further accumulated admiration. Given all that he did in so few years, Joseph scarcely had time to savor all the revelations that came to him, let alone take time to set forth, dissertation-like, all their implications carefully prepared, in serial sermons and metered lectures. That would be left to his successors, who as seers and revelators would correlate and clarify. President Joseph F. Smith did such regarding the words of Peter, as we see in Doctrine and Covenants 138.

One example of the numberless truths we have received through the Prophet Joseph concerns Enoch and his city, about whom we would know precious little if it were not for the Restoration scriptures. The few verses and biographical lines in the Bible are about genealogy and longevity and provide very little spiritual substance and instruction.

Paul tells us that Enoch was translated (he walked with God, who took him; Genesis 5:24) and before that Enoch "had this testimony, that he pleased God" (Hebrews 11:5). These biblical contributions are appreciated! Nevertheless, they can scarcely be compared with the stretching and deep substance in Moses 6 and 7 and Doctrine and Covenants 107:48–57.[8] Except for the Restoration, how would we know that not only was Enoch translated but so was the whole City of Enoch? This is the only known time in human history that a righteous people did not relapse.

Likewise, we learn through the Prophet Joseph Smith much more about the plurality of worlds—"worlds without number"—thereby advising us that Jesus is in effect the Lord of the Universe (Moses 1:33).

Among many others, either of these two examples (Enoch and the plurality of worlds) would have provided a sufficient field of specialized, spiritual scholarship to consume one for a whole lifetime. But the sheer abundance of such stunning truths in the Restoration by itself defied full delineation in the short time available to the Prophet Joseph Smith.

Furthermore, my appreciation for the Prophet Joseph is added upon when I ponder how the God-given revelations and instructions given to the Church also applied to Joseph himself and to his discipleship. This is no small consideration. Joseph's mortal mix of all "these things" was such that while Joseph was befriended by heavenly notables, he was also betrayed by some of his earthly friends. His receiving keys and gifts was real, but for him and Emma so was the painful loss of six of their eleven children. Granted, Joseph had revealed to him glimpses of far horizons—the first and the third estates—but these periodic glories occurred amid his arduous daily life as he struggled in the second estate.

At the same time the Prophet Joseph Smith was growing himself, he was tutoring other Church leaders. The capacity of the Prophet to inspire other remarkable leaders—strong men, often older than he, men such as Brigham Young and John Taylor, Wilford Woodruff, Lorenzo Snow, and so on—is significant, especially when those men suffered because of their devotion to the work to which they were called by the Prophet Joseph Smith, to whom and to which they remained so devoted. The tuition they paid for their followership and later leadership was, indeed, very high! Yet, they paid it gladly and praised the Prophet evermore.

President John Taylor declared: "I testify before God,

angels, and men, that he was a good, honorable, virtuous man—that his doctrines were good, scriptural, and wholesome—that his precepts were such as became a man of God—that his private and public character was unimpeachable—and that he lived and died as a man of God and a gentleman. This is my testimony."[9]

President Brigham Young bore witness: "Joseph Smith was not killed because he was deserving of it, nor because he was a wicked man; but because he was a virtuous man."[10]

President Young, for instance, also said, "I have been driven from my home five times; I have left my houses and lands and everything I had"—"and a good handsome property each time."[11] Five times he built homes in which he scarcely lived before being forced to leave them. How many lesser followers would be too discouraged to carry on even after just one such episode? The costs of discipleship were real and relentless!

There are the special testimonies from those like Oliver Cowdery. Oliver was closely associated with the Prophet during so much of his ministry, including the translation of the Book of Mormon. Though disaffected for several years, Oliver Cowdery came back, as we know. On his deathbed, the following episode occurred:

"Just before he breathed his last he [Oliver] asked to be raised up in bed so he could talk to the family and friends and he told them to live according to the teachings in the Book of Mormon and they would meet him in heaven. Then he said lay me down and let me fall asleep in the arms of Jesus, and he fell asleep without a struggle."[12]

Amid a customized combination of deprivations, stresses, and strains came imprisoned Joseph's lamentation: "Oh God, . . . where is the pavilion that covereth thy hiding place?" (D&C 121:1). It has a parallel in a persecuted and "in the stocks" Jeremiah (Jeremiah 20:2), who was deeply discouraged but nevertheless rallied:

"Then I said, I will not make mention of him, nor speak any more in his name. But his word was in mine heart as a burning fire shut up in my bones, and I was weary with forbearing, and I could not stay" (Jeremiah 20:9).

These words also surely describe latter-day defectors who were once loyal to the Prophet Joseph. Hence, we should ever bear in mind that prophets do experience their own real challenges.

Paul experienced much "in stripes, in imprisonments, in tumults, in labours, in watchings, in fastings" (2 Corinthians 6:5). Paul surely knew what it was to be beaten, to be "in perils by mine own country men . . . in the wilderness . . . among false brethren; in weariness and painfulness . . . in hunger . . . in cold" (2 Corinthians 11:24–28). During such times Paul, like Joseph Smith, had to attend to the overseership and "the care of all the churches" (2 Corinthians 11:28).

So it was that while Joseph received remarkable manifestations, along with these came constant vexations. True, there were periodic arrivals of heavenly messengers, but these were cruelly punctuated by the periodic arrivals of earthly mobs.

Joseph would have garnered many observations from his own experiences about human nature. No wonder, for instance, he spoke of how important it is for us to be long-suffering with each other.

Elder B. H. Roberts observed that a generous Prophet Joseph sometimes had "a too great tenacity in friendship for men he had once taken into his confidence after they had been proven unworthy of that friendship."[13]

Yet, no one was happier than Joseph when prodigals

returned, voting with their feet by traveling on the road of repentance toward reconciliation.

This slowness to recognize betrayal may have occurred because Joseph was simply unaware or precisely because he was trying to practice the doctrine of long-suffering. In any case, these interpersonal considerations were pressing in on him simultaneously with pressing concerns about the need to build temples and to administer essential temple ordinances in behalf of our ancestors—lest "the whole earth . . . be . . . wasted" (D&C 2:3; Malachi 4:6). But Joseph was also interested in doing what he could to ensure that an individual disciple's life was not "wasted." Such was the case of W. W. Phelps, whom the Prophet invited back into the Church so tenderly and lovingly:

"Dear Brother Phelps:— . . . It is true, that we have suffered much in consequence of your behavior—the cup of gall, already full enough for mortals to drink, was indeed filled to overflowing when you turned against us. One with whom we had oft taken sweet counsel together, and enjoyed many refreshing seasons from the Lord—'had it been an enemy, we could have borne it' . . .

"However, the cup has been drunk, the will of our Father has been done, and we are yet alive, for which we thank the Lord. . . .

"Believing your confession to be real, and your repentance genuine, I shall be happy once again to give you the right hand of fellowship, and rejoice over the returning prodigal. . . .

"'Come on, dear brother, since the war is past,
"'For friends at first, are friends again at last.'
"Yours as ever,
"Joseph Smith, Jun."[14]

Hence, the need for us, more than we do, to make

allowance, as in the case of Brother Phelps, for all that was going on simultaneously (and almost all the time) in Joseph's life, including kingdom building, establishing settlements of gathering, and sending out missionaries. It was all so unrelenting, including giving needed encouragement to fellow disciples and dictating and translating and contemplating what could be shared from the many revelations. There were no sabbaticals for Joseph, and even the reveries were short-lived.

Joseph's unusual capacity to be of good cheer in the midst of all "these things" is all the more commendable! This quality was special in view of the Lord's warning and confirming imagery: "Thine enemies prowl around thee" (D&C 122:6). The "very jaws of hell" seemed to gape at him (D&C 122:7). Does hell have its own halitosis? Joseph could tell us!

Noteworthy is the counsel of the Lord given at one of Joseph's lowest points (D&C 122). There was, after all, what the Lord Himself experienced—and incomparably. Hence, the query, "Art thou greater than He?" (D&C 122:8).

And there also was Job!

Having pled, Joseph never complained again.

Joseph's unusual resilience and his being of good cheer permitted him a special perspective, one buoyant and full of faith: "And as for the perils which I am called to pass through, they seem but a small thing to me, as the envy and wrath of man have been my common lot all the days of my life. . . . It has all become a second nature to me; . . . I shall triumph over all my enemies, for the Lord God hath spoken it" (D&C 127:2).

The Prophet Joseph's life was, therefore, anything but detached and monastic. He was both building a family and building a kingdom. He was growing himself while striving to help others do likewise, and, moreover, it was a portable process because of persecutions and drivings.

Amid considerations of personal safety, he was a father, husband, civic leader, translator, and Church leader of Zion's Camp and ensuing march. He was required to be a man of action and, at the same time, a man of contemplation. We can scarcely comprehend it!

No wonder he was wistful at times about how crowded his life was. Near the end of his eventful and revelation-filled ministry, Joseph seemed to realize how difficult it might be for others to understand him and his worth fully. "I don't blame any one for not believing my history. If I had not experienced what I have, I would not have believed it myself."[15]

Once the Prophet Joseph hoped aloud that he might so live amid his own heavy suffering that one day he could take his place among Abraham and the "ancients," hoping to "hold an even weight in the balances with them."[16] Joseph so triumphed, which is why we rightly sing of his being "crowned in the midst of the prophets of old."[17]

At the same time, he was mentoring the Twelve and needed them so much at his side. Yet, Joseph made a strategic decision to send a majority of the Twelve to England. They were needed to begin the harvest there, one upon which, as it turned out, the Church depended so much and so soon.

With difficulties and afflictions ever close at his heels, including real efforts to steal the plates, Joseph always made it to the top of the next ridge in pursuit of the Lord's agenda for the restored Church!

We do not know the precise schedule of his translation of particular portions of the Book of Mormon, but during some of those early days, the "choice seer," using "the gift and power of God" (2 Nephi 3:6; Omni 1:20), was translating, unawares, ancient Hebraisms, especially in the forepart of the Book of Mormon, or King Benjamin's great sermon, or the marvelous addition to the doctrine of the Atonement found in Alma 7:11–12. He translated these transcending truths and portions of the Bible but in the midst of a staccato of circumstances, including betrayals, mobs, and mockery.

Likewise, Joseph would have noted the first signs of potential problems in such men as Sidney Rigdon, who "exalted himself in his heart" (D&C 63:55; 93:44). Yet, Joseph did not censure prematurely for what had yet to happen. Thus, the constant challenge he faced to achieve balance between administering and ministering.

The book of Moses, with the marvelous passages about Enoch and the City of Enoch, came in June 1830 to February 1831. In that intermittent but tremendous effort, Joseph was also being introduced to the plurality of worlds—"millions of earths like this" (Moses 7:30). Also revealed to Joseph was Enoch's great, personalized acclamation to God, "Yet thou art there," as Enoch saw the God of heaven weep (Moses 7:28).

We can scarcely imagine—at this historical distance and as comfortable consumers of those revelations—the impact they would have had on Joseph as he received them in the midst of hurry and harassment.

To appreciate the Restoration even more fully, a fourth matter should be pondered: the context in which the Lord rolled it all forth, including its prophet.

It wouldn't have done much good to translate the Book of Mormon before there were printing presses and, more than that, before a printing capacity existed that extended to such locations as the Grandin Press in the obscure little town of Palmyra. How would the Book of Mormon have otherwise spread through the earth without such capacity now taken for granted? Computers and the Internet were a century and a half away!

The Restoration also very much required sufficient religious and political freedom in which the Lord's "strange act" could be brought forth (D&C 95:4). Obviously, the unique American Constitution was framed by those whom the Lord had "raised up" (D&C 101:80). Even in the American context, the Restoration was a close thing, with persecution, martyrdom, and the Saints being driven several times. But where else could the Restoration have occurred as safely, when, though in a favored nation, persecution and mobs would threaten to destroy or evict the restored Church? Hence, this promised land needed to be big enough in the face of mounting persecution to provide for escape and exodus. Such happened when the Saints moved to the western mountains and thereby became, as prophesied, "a mighty people"—for Joseph had declared, as Anson Call remembered, "Some of you will live to go and assist in making settlements and build cities and see the Saints become a mighty people in the midst of the Rocky Mountains."[18]

The Saints' being driven regionally from time to time was grim enough, but it would have been even more so to have them hopelessly and finally cornered elsewhere! Hence, the importance of America's rugged but nevertheless accommodating western frontier.

Furthermore, given the earlier hemisphere history of the people who produced sacred plates, translated, and buried them, clearly, the Western Hemisphere needed to be the place of finding.

Think, too, of how the language of reformed Egyptian required a rich receiving language such as English, with its variety and nuances. What was on the golden plates flowed best into a golden language! Feasting on the gospel is greatly facilitated by its "enough and to spare" abundance (D&C 104:17).

Likewise, because the gospel in the last dispensation would be spread from this place to all the world, a nation with sufficient opportunities and economic strength was needed to host such a restored kingdom. In the rhythm of the Restoration, the gospel was to go first to the rich and then to the poor, and the Lord would finally "hasten" his work in its time (D&C 88:73). America, with all its imperfections, has served and now serves well as that stable host nation.

The few foregoing examples remind us that not only does the Lord see the end from the beginning but He also sees the middle. The emerging of His kingdom required certain conditions required for that restoration to succeed. Indeed, the Lord had prepared a place, a time, and a season. He also prepared the Prophet, through whom all the "marvelous work and a wonder" would unfold—even amid so many challenges and difficulties (2 Nephi 25:17).

Viewed from my sunset days, the foothills of lesser things which were part of the Restoration merge into the vaulting doctrinal peaks. The colors and hues actually seem to sharpen. The composite silhouette stands out in bold relief, giving the latter-day disciple a striking but subduing sense of the breathtaking range of the glorious Restoration. Even more spectacular in my sunset days, that range has evoked the testimony of Christ that I hope resonates throughout the foregoing pages.

NOTES

NOTE TO PREAMBLE, *page 1*
    1. *Teachings of the Prophet Joseph Smith,* 220.

NOTES TO CHAPTER ONE, *page 8*
    1. *Mormon Doctrine,* 218.
    2. Conference Report, October 1918, 59.
    3. *An Essay on Man,* in *Oxford Dictionary of Quotations,* 383.
    4. "Reflections," 5.
    5. These are *not* scripture, but as with other apocrypha *may* contain things "that are true" (D&C 91:1, 5). Pseudepigraphic and apocryphal sources do contain "some truths" and may be "useful," even though these texts were written by others long after the time of those whose names they bear: such is the case with some pseudepigraphic works about Enoch (LDS Bible Dictionary, s.v. "Enoch," 665; s.v. "Pseudepigrapha," 755).
    6. *Journal of Discourses,* 13:280.
    7. Bury, *History of Greece,* 264.

NOTES TO CHAPTER TWO, *page 19*
    1. *Story of Philosophy,* 2.
    2. *Teachings of the Prophet Joseph Smith,* 121.
    3. *Politics at God's Funeral,* 11.
    4. *Journal of Discourses,* 3:158.
    5. *Journal of Discourses,* 22:262–63; 1 Corinthians 1:26.
    6. *Teachings of the Prophet Joseph Smith,* 220.
    7. *Hymns,* no. 272.
    8. *Hymns,* no. 292; see also D&C 45:13.

9. Smith, *Gospel Doctrine*, 203.

10. *Treasury of Great Poems*, 488.

11. Goldsmith, *Worlds Unnumbered*, xiv.

12. Hawking, *Black Holes and Baby Universes*, 99.

13. Powell, "Up against the Wall," 19.

14. Chandler, "Largest Structure," 22.

15. McMillan and Chaisson, *Astronomy Today*, 559.

16. Strauss, "Cluster of Galaxies," A1.

17. Barrow and Tipler, "Anthropic Cosmological Principle," Foreword.

18. Will, *Pursuit of Happiness*, 228.

19. "Thanks to the Lord for His Blessings," 88.

20. "At the Summit of the Ages," 74.

NOTES TO CHAPTER THREE, *page 34*

1. *Teachings of the Prophet Joseph Smith*, 220.

2. *Hymns*, no. 131.

3. Lewis, *Weight of Glory*, 14.

4. *Teachings of the Prophet Joseph Smith*, 220.

5. *World's Last Night*, 10–11.

6. *Teachings of the Prophet Joseph Smith*, 343.

7. Genovese, "Pilgrim's Progress," 38; italics added.

8. *Teachings of the Prophet Joseph Smith*, 354.

9. Ehat and Cook, *Words of Joseph Smith*, 183.

10. LDS Bible Dictionary, s.v. "repentance," 760.

11. Jessee, *Personal Writings of Joseph Smith*, 387; punctuation standardized.

NOTES TO CHAPTER FOUR, *page 46*

1. *Teachings of the Prophet Joseph Smith*, 241.

2. *Teachings of the Prophet Joseph Smith*, 241.

3. Quoted in Bullock, *Hitler and Stalin*, 976.

4. *March of Folly*, 381.

5. Flexner, *Washington*, xvi.

6. *Teachings of the Prophet Joseph Smith*, 51.

7. *Journal of Discourses*, 9:293.

8. *Journal of Discourses*, 9:125–26.

9. *Journal of Discourses,* 8:367.

10. Conference Report, April 1966, 75.

Notes to Chapter Five, *page 59*

1. *C. S. Lewis Poems,* 118.

2. *Teachings of the Prophet Joseph Smith,* 343.

3. *Hymns,* no. 165.

Notes to Chapter Six, *page 70*

1. The Prophet Joseph added the last, six-word clause as he reviewed the wording of the revelation.

2. *C. S. Lewis Poems,* 118.

3. Hyde, *Journal of Discourses,* 7:149–50.

4. *Journal of Discourses,* 7:275.

5. *Instant Memory,* 3.

6. *Instant Memory,* 3.

7. *Works of Walter Bagehot,* 1:306–7.

8. *Seven Deadly Sins Today,* 175.

9. *De-Moralization of Society,* 261–63.

10. *Lessons of History,* 35–36.

11. *Passing of the Modern Age,* 169.

12. Umehara, "Civilization of the Forest."

Notes to Chapter Seven, *page 80*

1. *Poetry of Robert Frost,* 225.

2. *Severe Mercy,* 202.

3. *Teachings of the Prophet Joseph Smith,* 220.

4. *Things Past,* 74.

5. *Hymns,* no. 272.

6. *Hymns,* no. 131.

7. Conference Report, April 1900, 41.

Notes to Chapter Eight, *page 92*

1. *History of the Church,* 4:42.

2. Pratt, *Key to the Science of Theology,* 61.

3. The headnote to John 7 indicates the kinsmen did not believe in Jesus.

4. Quoted in Packer, *Teach Ye Diligently,* 304.

5. *Journal of Discourses,* 1:90.

6. *Journal of Discourses*, 1:313.

7. *Hymns*, no. 19.

8. Young to West.

9. *Teachings of the Prophet Joseph Smith*, 176.

10. *Journal of Discourses*, 3:316.

11. Quoted in Packer, *That All May Be Edified*, 340.

12. Wilson, *Moral Sense*, 163.

13. Watson, *Manuscript History of Brigham Young*.

NOTES TO CHAPTER NINE, *page 105*

1. "Discourse," 1.

2. *Discourses of Wilford Woodruff*, 288–89.

3. *Journal of Discourses*, 4:135–36.

4. *Journal of Discourses*, 3:368.

5. *Journal of Discourses*, 3:372.

6. *Teachings of the Prophet Joseph Smith*, 326.

7. *Journal of Discourses*, 2:137.

8. Ehat and Cook, *Words of Joseph Smith*, 183.

9. *History of the Church*, 6:314.

10. *Teachings of the Prophet Joseph Smith*, 220.

11. Ehat and Cook, *Words of Joseph Smith*, 372; punctuation standardized.

12. *Teachings of the Prophet Joseph Smith*, 223.

13. Ehat and Cook, *Words of Joseph Smith*, 370; spelling and punctuation standardized.

NOTES TO CHAPTER TEN, *page 115*

1. *Teachings of the Prophet Joseph Smith*, 296.

2. Jones, *Emma's Glory and Sacrifice*, 44.

3. "Trial of Elder Rigdon," 650.

4. *Teachings of the Prophet Joseph Smith*, 113.

5. *Journal of Discourses*, 24:197–98.

6. *Teachings of the Prophet Joseph Smith*, 368.

7. Quoted in Cannon, Journal, 7 January 1898, 29.

8. "Enoch, about whom there are only seven verses in the Bible, becomes a major figure in Restoration scripture. There are eighteen times as many column inches about Enoch in the

Restoration scriptures as we have in the few verses on him in the Bible" (Robert J. Matthews, letter to author, 12 August 1988).

9. *Gospel Kingdom*, 355.

10. *Journal of Discourses*, 1:40.

11. *Journal of Discourses*, 7:205; 13:318.

12. Cowdery to Young; capitalization and punctuation standardized.

13. *Comprehensive History of the Church*, 2:358.

14. *History of the Church*, 4:163–64.

15. *History of the Church*, 6:317.

16. Jessee, *Personal Writings of Joseph Smith*, 395; spelling standardized.

17. *Hymns*, no. 27.

18. *History of the Church*, 5:85.

SOURCES

Bagehot, Walter. *The Works of Walter Bagehot*. Edited by Forrest Morgan. Hartford, Conn.: The Travelers Insurance Company, 1889.

Barrow, John D., and Frank J. Tipler. *The Anthropic Cosmological Principle*. Oxford: Clarendon, 1986.

Bullock, Alan. *Hitler and Stalin: Parallel Lives*. New York: Alfred A. Knopf, 1992.

Bury, J. B. *A History of Greece*. New York: The Modern Library, 1913.

Chandler, David L. "Largest Structure Found in Universe Defies Explanation." *Sacramento Union*, 19 November 1989, 22.

Conference Reports. Salt Lake City: The Church of Jesus Christ of Latter-day Saints, 1899–2000.

Durant, Will. *The Story of Philosophy*. New York: Simon and Schuster, 1927.

Durant, Will, and Ariel Durant. *The Lessons of History*. New York: Simon and Schuster, 1968.

Durham, G. Homer. *The Discourses of Wilford Woodruff*. Salt Lake City: Bookcraft, 1990.

Ehat, Andrew, and Lyndon Cook. *The Words of Joseph Smith*. Provo, Utah: Grandin, 1991.

Fairlie, Henry. *The Seven Deadly Sins Today*. Washington, D. C.: New Republic Books, 1978.

Flexner, James Thomas. *Washington: The Indispensable Man*. New York: Plume, 1974.

Frost, Robert. *The Poetry of Robert Frost*. Edited by Edward

Connery Lathem. New York: Holt, Rinehart and Winston, 1974.

Genovese, Eugene D. "Pilgrim's Progress." *New Republic,* 11 May 1992, 38.

Goldsmith, Donald. *Worlds Unnumbered: The Search for Extrasolar Planets.* Sausalito, Calif.: University Science Books, 1997.

Harrington, Michael. *The Politics at God's Funeral.* New York: Holt, Rinehart and Winston, 1983.

Hawking, Stephen W. *Black Holes and Baby Universes.* New York: Bantam Books, 1993.

Himmelfarb, Gertrude. *The De-Moralization of Society.* New York: Alfred A. Knopf, 1995.

Hinckley, Gordon B. "Thanks to the Lord for His Blessings." *Ensign,* May 1999, 88.

———. "At the Summit of the Ages." *Ensign,* November 1999, 74.

Hymns of The Church of Jesus Christ of Latter-day Saints. Salt Lake City: The Church of Jesus Christ of Latter-day Saints, 1985.

Instant Memory: The Automatic Memory System. Pacific Palisades, Calif.: The Institute of Advanced Thinking, 1972.

Jessee, Dean C., ed. *The Personal Writings of Joseph Smith.* Salt Lake City: Deseret Book, 1984.

Jones, Gracia N. *Emma's Glory and Sacrifice: A Testimony.* Hurricane, Utah: Homestead Publishers, 1987.

Journal of Discourses. 26 vols. London: Latter-day Saints' Book Depot, 1854–86.

Lewis, C. S. *C. S. Lewis Poems.* Edited by Walter Hooper. New York: Harcourt Brace Jovanovich, 1977.

———. *The Weight of Glory.* Grand Rapids, Mich.: William B. Eerdmans, 1977.

———. *The World's Last Night and Other Essays by C. S. Lewis.* New York: Harvest Books, 1973.

Lukacs, John. *The Passing of the Modern Age.* New York: Harper and Row, 1970.

Matthews, Robert J. Letter to author, 12 August 1988.

McConkie, Bruce R. *Mormon Doctrine.* 2d ed. Salt Lake City: Bookcraft, 1966.

McMillan, Steve, and Eric J. Chaisson. *Astronomy Today.* Upper Saddle River, N.J.: Prentice Hall, 1993.

Muggeridge, Malcolm. *Things Past.* New York: William Morrow and Company, 1979.

The Oxford Dictionary of Quotations. 2d ed. London: Oxford University Press, 1975.

Packer, Boyd K. *Teach Ye Diligently.* Salt Lake City: Deseret Book, 1975.

———. *That All May Be Edified.* Salt Lake City: Bookcraft, 1982.

———. *The Holy Temple.* Salt Lake City: Bookcraft, 1980.

Powell, Corey S. "Up against the Wall." *Scientific American,* February 1990, 18–19.

Pratt, Parley P. *Key to the Science of Theology.* Salt Lake City: Deseret Book, 1978.

Roberts, B. H. *A Comprehensive History of The Church of Jesus Christ of Latter-day Saints, Century One.* 6 vols. Salt Lake City: The Church of Jesus Christ of Latter-day Saints, 1930.

Smith, Joseph. *History of The Church of Jesus Christ of Latter-day Saints.* Edited by B. H. Roberts. 2d ed. rev. 7 vols. Salt Lake City: The Church of Jesus Christ of Latter-day Saints, 1932–51.

———. *Teachings of the Prophet Joseph Smith.* Selected by Joseph Fielding Smith. Salt Lake City: Deseret Book, 1938.

Smith, Joseph F. *Gospel Doctrine.* Salt Lake City: Deseret Book, 1939.

Snow, Lorenzo. In George Q. Cannon, Journal, 7 January 1898. Journal in private possession.

Solzhenitsyn, Aleksandr. "Reflections on the Eve of the Twenty-first Century." In *At Century's End: Great Minds Reflect on Our Times.* Edited by Nathan P. Gardels. La Jolla, Calif.: Alti Publishing, 1996.

Strauss, Stephen. "Clusters of Galaxies Form Pattern like Honeycomb, Astronomy Teams Find." *Globe and Mail,* 5 February 1990.

Taylor, John. "Discourse by Elder John Taylor." *Deseret News,* 28 July 1874, 1.

———. *The Gospel Kingdom.* Salt Lake City: Bookcraft, 1987.

"Trial of Elder Rigdon." *Times and Seasons,* 15 September 1844, 650.

Tuchman, Barbara W. *March of Folly: From Troy to Vietnam.* New York: Alfred A. Knopf, 1984.

Umehara, Takeshi. "The Civilization of the Forest: Ancient Japan Shows Postmodernism the Way." In *At Century's End: Great Minds Reflect on Our Times.* Edited by Nathan P. Gardels. La Jolla, Calif.: ALTI Publishing, 1995.

Untermeyer, Louis, ed. *A Treasury of Great Poems English and American.* New York: Simon and Schuster, 1955.

Vanauken, Sheldon. *A Severe Mercy.* New York: Bantam, 1979.

Watson, Elden J., comp. *Manuscript History of Brigham Young, 1846–1847.* Salt Lake City: Elden J. Watson, 1971.

Will, George F. *The Pursuit of Happiness, and Other Sobering Thoughts.* New York: Harper & Row, 1978.

Wilson, James Q. *The Moral Sense.* New York: Free Press, 1993.

Young, Brigham. Letter to Bishop C. W. West, 29 September 1857. Brigham Young Letterpress Copy Book. Typescript. Archives of The Church of Jesus Christ of Latter-day Saints, Salt Lake City.

Young, Lucy Cowdery. Letter to Brigham Young, 7 March 1887. Archives of The Church of Jesus Christ of Latter-day Saints, Salt Lake City.

INDEX

INDEX